The House on Neptune

Confessions of a Resident Alien

By Brian Robbins

Happy Birthday, Mark!

Copyright © 2009 by Brian Robbins

The House on Neptune
Confessions of a Resident Alien
by Brian Robbins

Printed in the United States of America

ISBN 978-1-60791-445-7

All rights reserved solely by the author. The author guarantees all contents are original and do not infringe upon the legal rights of any other person or work. No part of this book may be reproduced in any form without the permission of the author. The views expressed in this book are not necessarily those of the publisher.

Unless otherwise indicated, Bible quotations are taken from The NIV Version of the Bible. Copyright © 2002 by Zondervan.

www.xulonpress.com

This book is dedicated to my wife, who shares my hope in the house on Neptune, and whose companionship makes it a lot easier to be so far from home. I love you, Carey.

"If only for this life we have hope in Christ,
we are to be pitied more than all men."
—Paul, 1 Corinthians 15:19

Table of Contents

prologue: strangers in a strange land xi
earth: your home away from home 15
christians: on a mission from God 27
the church: aliens unanimous.................................47
you and your planet: vessels in need of repair.......65
evangelism: we come in peace................................91
suffering: breathing the air of a hostile world......115
ministers: take me to your leader.........................137
death: resistance is futile......................................159
life: searching for signs..175
heaven: the house on Neptune 197
epilogue: arriving on Neptune 211
acknowledgements..215

prologue: strangers in a strange land

First, let me explain the title.

My wife and I are waiting for our house to be built, and when it is finished, we will live on Neptune. Neptune Avenue, I mean. The streets in our town all have names that are nautical and alphabetical, and when the city fathers had to come up with a name for the street between Mast and Oar, Neptune is apparently the best they could do. In mythology, Neptune was the Roman name for the god of the sea, and the Romans named a distant planet after him. This is fitting, because for most of my life I have felt like an outsider, like I don't really belong, like maybe I'm from another planet. At least now my address will reflect what I've always suspected.

I am a Christian, and, what is worse, a pastor, so I'm not exaggerating when I say that I'm different. Everyone knows it. When people find out who I am and what I do, they stop being themselves. They stop talking about whatever they were talking about, and try to imagine what a pastor talks about when he is not in his office, communing with the Almighty. They try especially hard not to swear, and apologize when they do. They seem to fear that I might be some sort of heavenly spy, sent by God to see what they are up to, and to report any suspicious behavior back to Headquarters. It can be pretty amusing, but it is also very isolating. Despite what many people think, pastors are not hatched from an egg or produced full-grown at a pastor factory. I am just a normal guy, so normal that I even had a childhood. Like many people's childhoods, mine consisted largely of trying to convince the world that I was cool. The desire to be part of the crowd, to fit in, is as deeply ingrained in pastors as in anyone else. But we are definitely in the wrong profession for it. Shortly after enrolling in seminary, I realized that my days of being treated like a normal person were gone for good, and I have to admit that, at first, I resented this.

But then I began to discover something in the Bible. As a Christian and a pastor, I take the Bible very seriously. I believe God has spoken to people by giving us this one book that contains everything he wants to say to us. We can trust the Bible and build our lives on its teachings. Most Christians know this, even though we don't always live like it. Lately, though, the Bible has been making me a little uncomfortable, and I have been at this long enough to know that when this happens, it's not God's Word that needs to change, it's me. I've begun to notice quite a few places where the Bible calls me and my fellow Christians names like "stranger" and "alien."

Although I was born and raised on planet Earth, it says that I am not truly a citizen here, but rather a sort of long-term visitor. Furthermore, it says that if I really believed and embraced this truth, I would be better equipped for this life and better prepared for the next. The more I read, the more I wonder if I have had the wrong goal all along. Maybe fitting in is just the opposite of what I'm supposed to be doing. Maybe I would be better off seeing myself the way the Bible sees me, as an alien who is a long way from home.

That is what this book is about: embracing our identity as aliens on planet Earth. It is about living, and living well, in a place where we don't belong. If you feel completely comfortable with your life as it is, if you feel that you've arrived at your destination and you're satisfied with things as they are, then it probably isn't for you. This book is written for Jesus' followers who are still on the journey, by a fellow traveler who is also on the journey, and is tired of trying to build mansions at every rest stop. It is for Christians who feel that life is not what it should be, and want to know why. We believe that Jesus is the answer, and yet we still have questions. Somehow, trusting Christ has not solved all of our problems. What are we missing? My sense is that many Christians secretly feel that there must be more to life, and are afraid to say it. Sadly, they are unaware that the Bible has an answer for them. What we are missing, very simply, is home. We are stuck between two worlds: the one we have always known and the one that beckons us from a distance, which is both strange and familiar at the same time. We will get there someday; but in the meantime, how should we live? That is the question explored in these pages. May God use what is written in them, for your good and His glory.

> Brian Robbins
> Lincoln City, Oregon
> November 2005

Chapter One

earth: your home away from home

Carey and I are homeless. We have been for several months now.

Ours is not the kind of homelessness that comes from poverty, but the kind that comes from transition. We have left one place and are not quite settled in another. This summer we moved to a new town, where we are staying with a family of strangers. They have opened their home to us while ours is being built, which is very kind of them. They share their space, their meals, and their time with us; if you have to be homeless, you really couldn't ask for a better situation. But still, it is not our home. No matter how hard we try, we can't totally relax and be ourselves here. Something just doesn't feel right.

I suppose it's not really fair to compare ourselves with real homeless people, with the millions of people around the world who have nowhere to go and no one to help. Life is much easier for us. We sleep in a bed and eat warm meals, and we have somewhere to go when it rains, which is no small thing here on the Oregon coast. But in one important way, we feel very much like the people you see spending their days on park benches and sleeping under bridges. Like them, we don't know where we belong. We don't have a place that's ours. We keep ourselves occupied during the day with work, play, exercise, whatever we can find. Because I am the new guy on staff at our church, we are invited to eat at other people's houses a lot, which gives our host family a break and helps us get acquainted with our new surroundings. But at the end of the day, we don't belong anywhere. You'd be surprised how exhausting it is. This summer was the first summer in a long time that we haven't gone camping; we were just too tired. We felt like we were camping all the time, and the idea of packing up the car and going somewhere else to live out of a backpack was completely unappealing. Life goes on, and good things are happening, in our lives and our jobs. But we are ready, very ready, for our home.

Meanwhile, as I said, our home is being built. We have lived as renters up until now, so this will be the first home we have ever owned. For a long time, we didn't think we would ever be able to buy a house, but now it is happening. We drive down Neptune Avenue every once in a while to take a look at it, although at this point there is not much to see. We talk about what it will be like when we get to move in. We imagine how it will look when it is finished, and we try to picture our lives there, but those images are blurry. In some ways, the house on Neptune is the great hope that keeps us going through this time of transition, but in other ways it seems very unreal. Building is a slow process in this rainy place. Some days it feels like we will always be homeless, like we had just better get used to someone else's food, someone else's house, someone else's bed. It feels like the house will never be more than a foundation with some pieces of soggy wood sticking up. But then we get glimpses. We'll be looking at the floor plan, picking out paint colors or something, and we'll be struck with the fact that this whole thing is really happening. The house on Neptune is real, and we really are going to live there. It is only a matter of time.

Growing up as a Christian, I have always been told that I should look for the lessons God is trying to teach me in my struggles, rather than just sit around complaining and waiting for things to get better. A couple of weeks ago, a light bulb went on and I realized that this is what I should be doing in my current time of transition. "What is God teaching me as I wait for the house on Neptune?" I asked. There are probably many lessons that I am missing, but I have stumbled across one that is fairly significant: waiting for the house on Neptune is a metaphor for my entire life, and the lives of everyone I know. Let me explain:

Everyone I know, including myself, is waiting for something. We all have this sense of not having arrived, and we place our hope in some future event or accomplishment to finally make life good. "When this thing happens," we tell ourselves, "I'll be able to relax. Things will really be good after that." Look around and ask yourself how many people you know who are truly content. I don't think I know any. As a pastor, I have had the privilege of knowing people who have dedicated their lives to praying and seeking God. Those people, compared to the rest of us, usually do have some measure of peace. But even they are not truly *at* peace. We all feel like something is missing. In this way, I'm coming to see that my current state of homelessness is actually not that unusual. It is just an exaggerated experience of the way that we all feel, somewhere deep down in our hearts, pretty much all the time. This sense of longing for more is a universal human experience. And, whether or not we know it, we are longing for something specific. We are longing for home.

I am talking, of course, about heaven. In our culture, it has become very unfashionable to talk about heaven. This is because talking about heaven implies that there might be something really wrong with earth, and that we might need a great big God to rescue us from whatever is wrong. It is much more socially acceptable to believe that with a little effort, passing the right laws and convincing some of the especially mean people to just be nice, we could make this world into everything we want it to be. When someone believes this, they do not want to hear about heaven; they want to hear a plan to help people start being perfect without anyone having to die on a cross. To them, hoping for heaven is like admitting defeat—it is the coward's way out. If they are honest, they will have to admit that every attempt to create an earthly paradise in the last few millennia has failed miserably, but they still believe the solution could be right around the corner.

It makes sense for people like that not to talk about heaven. Lately, though, something different is happening, at least among the people I know. Lately it seems that it is the church, the people who have already cried out for God's help, who don't talk about heaven as much. I don't know why; maybe we finally clued in to the fact that it wasn't cool anymore. Christians, after all, are a little bit like I was in junior high—constantly wanting to be accepted, but always a little bit behind the fashion of the times. Eventually, we pick up on the same trends that sweep through the rest of culture; it just takes us a little longer. Whatever the reason, we seem more reluctant to dwell upon the things of eternity than our parents and grandparents were. Don't get me wrong; there are still many good things happening in the American church. We are still talking about victory over sin and addiction, about healthy relationships, peace of mind, and selfless love. Those are all good things, things Jesus can bring into a person's life right here and now. They are a part of the gospel, the good news of new life in Jesus Christ. But they are not the whole gospel, because the whole gospel includes the fact that this new life is eternal. Read the New Testament with open eyes, and you will see that the hope of eternal life is everywhere; it is absolutely central to the Christian faith. No matter what other good things we're doing, if we stop talking about heaven, we have stopped presenting the world with authentic Christianity.

Previous generations had no problem talking about heaven. They were not ashamed. You don't have to look any further than the songs they sang:

> Some glad morning, when this life is o'er, I'll
>   fly away
> To a land on God's celestial shore, I'll fly away
> I'll fly away, O Glory, I'll fly away
> When I die, hallelujah, by and by, I'll fly away

or this one:

> This world is not my home; I'm just a-passin'
>   through
> My treasures are laid up somewhere beyond the
>   blue,
> The angels beckon me from Heaven's open
>   door,
> And I can't feel at home in this world anymore

Carey and I were watching a movie a few weeks ago that took place in the time of the Civil War. There was a scene in a church, and all the people were singing this old spiritual, with no instruments, in four-part harmony. I don't remember all of it, but I remember the last line of the chorus: "And I don't care to stay here long." The rest of the movie was largely a waste of my time, but I was glad I saw it just for that scene. There was something about a group of Jesus' followers, gathered together for worship, with pain and destruction all around them, singing about how they would much rather be in heaven, that stuck with me. For the rest of that week, I caught myself humming that old song as I faced the daily struggles of life. It gave me a feeling of peace, like everything had been put in its proper place, because it reminded me that everything I was dealing with was temporary, and would someday pass away.

I realize there are some Christians who are just as offended by this as the rest of our culture, and for a good reason. They are afraid that daydreaming about heaven will keep us from meeting the needs of the world around us. They think it makes us lazy and passive, and distracts us from making a real contribution where it matters. They even have a saying to describe the problem they are talking about. They call it "being too heavenly minded to be any earthly good." But it's easy to be misled by sayings like that, which sound clever but don't come from scripture. The truth is, there is more than one way that someone could be called a "heavenly minded" person. It is certainly possible to be caught up in obscure theological issues that don't really matter, or to daydream our lives away and waste time that should have been spent on things that help people and glorify God. Some people think and talk about God and salvation and eternity all the time, but in the end their lives produce very little real fruit. That is definitely an error we want to avoid.

But there is another way we can be "heavenly minded": we can give our time and our effort to things of eternal value. Instead of just theorizing about spiritual things, we can take action, but action that is focused on the Kingdom of God. Because God and people last forever, heaven is not the opposite of earth—the most important things about earth will carry over into eternity. This means that the two are not necessarily in competition. What is good for heaven is good for earth. If someone is focused on what matters most in eternity, they will do all sorts of good here on earth, as a by-product of their heavenly-minded efforts.

The truth is, most of us are a long way from having to worry about going off the deep end and wasting our lives on spiritual abstractions. If you are like me, then it is much more likely that you will fall into the opposite error: getting lost in the shallow end, and being deceived into thinking that earthly good is the greatest good. As American Christians, we live in the busiest, shallowest culture in human history. Most of us could cut out several hours of activity from our weekly schedules, spend all of our new-found time in prayer and contemplation of spiritual things, and still not run the risk of being too heavenly minded. Instead, many of us may someday find that we were too earthly minded to do anything of real significance. We will see that when we stopped dreaming about heaven, we lost sight of what matters here on earth.

The apostle Paul is a great example of someone who was always mindful of heaven, and yet did an incredible amount of good with his life here on earth. Paul was one of the first Christians, a man who met Jesus, was transformed by God's forgiveness and grace, and dedicated his life to spreading the Gospel. He also thought about heaven all the time. As you read his letters, you get the impression that heaven was as real to him as earth was (it probably helped that God allowed him to see heaven—see 2 Corinthians 12). His entire focus was on his eternal destiny, and the eternal destiny of others. And yet he had tremendous impact. Paul was used by God to plant many of the churches of the first century of Christianity, and, under the inspiration of God's Holy Spirit, to write about half of the New Testament of the Bible. Not bad for a guy with his head in the clouds.

One time, Paul was writing to a group of young Christians in a town called Philippi. He wanted them to understand that not everyone would share their beliefs and values, so they needed to be wise about who they imitated:

> For, as I have often told you before and now say again even with tears, many live as enemies of the cross of Christ. Their destiny is destruction, their god is their stomach, and their glory is in their shame. Their mind is on earthly things. *But our citizenship is in heaven.* And we eagerly await a Savior from there, the Lord Jesus Christ, who, by the power that enables him to bring everything under his control, will transform our lowly bodies so that they will be like his glorious body (Php. 3:18-21, italics added).

Paul knew that people respond in different ways to the universal human experience of longing. Some people, alienated from God by their sin, refuse the offer of forgiveness, reconciliation, and eternal life through Jesus Christ. They convince themselves that there is no God, and no heaven, and ultimately they make this the truth of their eternal lives. In the meantime, their only option is to look for heaven on earth. This is, of course, ultimately an exercise in frustration, but people are surprisingly stubborn, and can keep themselves occupied for entire lifetimes trying to carve out a little private paradise in the middle of a sinful, self-destructing world. The goal of their lives becomes the satisfaction of their various appetites, and they do all sorts of things that, as my grandma would say, they should be ashamed of, in pursuit of this goal. Their destiny is destruction, their god is their stomach, and their glory is in their shame.

But Christians, followers of Jesus, are not like that. Our citizenship is in heaven. Christians live differently, because we believe differently. We believe that we belong somewhere else. When you are a citizen of a country, that country is not only your home when you are there, but its rules and customs shape your life even when you are elsewhere. That's how it is supposed to be for us. We are supposed to believe so deeply in our heavenly citizenship that we live in this world as visitors. I know that is uncomfortable. It is also biblical. And it is exciting. It means that we can be okay with the universal experience of longing. Of course this world doesn't satisfy us. It isn't home. It's okay that we sometimes find it disappointing—we don't belong here anyway.

Jesus seemed to assume that people have a built-in hope of heaven when he said to his followers "Do not be afraid. Trust in God; trust also in me. In my Father's house are many rooms; if it were not so, I would have told you" (John 14:1,2, NIV). *If it were not so, I would have told you!* Jesus is saying, "Of course. Of course there is a heaven, a place where you will feel at home, just as you have always hoped there was. If your hopes were going to be disappointed, I would have let you know right away." Then he went on to say, "I am going there to prepare a place for you. And if I go and prepare a place for you, I will come back and take you to be with me that you also may be where I am." (vv 2,3). Our home is being built. Yes, Jesus came to bring us victory over sin, healthy relationships, and peace on earth. Mostly, though, he came to bring us home.

That being said, I should make it clear that this is not a book about heaven. There are other books which examine scripture and shed light on the things we can look forward to for the rest of eternity. I would encourage you to find them and read them. This book is about earth, about how a person might live this short life on earth if they have truly received life that is eternal. It is a book that seeks to answer one simple question: What if you truly believed that, as a follower of Jesus, you don't belong here, because your citizenship is in heaven? What if you are really a sort of visitor from a distant planet, far from home, making the best of things here in the place you happen to find yourself? What difference would it make if that were true?

I will tell you the difference it is making for me: it is changing everything about how I see the world, and everything about how I live in the world. Not all at once, of course, but over time. I can already say, even at the beginning of my journey, that it is a wonderfully freeing thing to realize that I am not at home in this world. I think you will discover the same thing. It is my hope that many of Christ's followers are getting tired of trying to be like the world around us. Perhaps it's time for us to admit, even embrace, the fact that we don't fit in here. Christians are never going to be cool, and maybe we should give up trying. Maybe we should even make it our goal to be different; maybe that is exactly what the world needs. The following chapters will examine life on earth from this new perspective, imagining how we would think, feel, and live if we believed that we were visitors, passing through on our way to heaven. I know that some of us are not really ready for this: it is frightening to think that we are citizens of somewhere we have never been. To be honest, some of us have worked hard to blend into our current surroundings, and we are not quite ready to let that dream die. That is okay. God takes us as we are. But if we are Christians at all, on some level we must believe that God is real, and that heaven is real, or we wouldn't have bothered with this whole thing in the first place. All God wants to do is take that seed of faith and make it grow, until the thing we can't see is just as real to us as the things we already see. It's like I keep telling Carey: The house on Neptune is real, and we really are going to live there. It is only a matter of time.

Chapter Two

Christians: on a mission from God

I don't watch much television. As a pastor, I probably wouldn't admit it if I did, because some people have strong feelings about that. Honestly, though, it's not a major part of my life. My own TV is currently in storage, but every once in a while Carey and I flip through the channels at our hosts' house in search of some mindless entertainment. We usually find some. We have noticed something unusual about this particular television season. If you didn't know, TV has seasons, like professional sports. The life of a television writer, apparently, is somewhat comparable in its demands to that of a professional hockey player, and so they are only able to work for about six months out of the year. That is why we have summer reruns, which start in April or so. This is a chance to re-live all of the life-changing moments from the first time the shows were aired. Then, in the fall, there is the feeling of great anticipation as the hard-working writers return to their craft, and new and better shows are unveiled. It's a beautiful system. Anyway, for some reason, this season there appears to be a renewed interest in one of the classic themes of human drama: slimy aliens taking over the world. You can find variations on this theme on several networks, although I suppose it is possible that by the time this book is published, if it is published at all, some of these shows may be cancelled. It may be that the uncultured masses will fail to properly appreciate their depth and subtlety, opting instead to spend their viewing time watching real people make new friends and then stab them in the back for money. Great art is rarely appreciated in its own time.

As far as I can tell, this is how these shows work: The aliens want our planet, because back home on Zalcon-4 they elected too many Republicans and recklessly depleted all their natural resources. But now they have learned their lesson, and don't want to lay waste to our wetlands and national forests with their heat rays during the takeover. So, instead of an all-out war, they have concocted an evil scheme: they will infiltrate our cities and towns by actually invading human bodies and becoming just like us. They look like us, talk like us, and even eat cheeseburgers in an attempt to blend in, although they prefer human flesh. Invariably, a few normal people (and by normal I mean good-looking scientists who carry guns) begin to suspect that something funny is going on, because every once in a while someone will disappear and leave nothing but a puddle of slime. But no one will believe them, and so this small group is left alone to get to the bottom of the mystery and stop the alien invasion. Meanwhile, one of their number, often an attractive blonde woman or an actor who has perfected his menacing glare, will begin to act strangely. At first it's just little things: disappearing at odd times, never needing to sleep, stuff like that. Puddles of slime continue to make regular appearances, and then one day, just before a commercial break, this person stares right at the camera, gives a menacing glare, and his or her eyes glow green. And you jump out of your chair and shout "I knew it! The alien!" But of course, no one listens. The team keeps following the clues, but time is running out. Meanwhile, their friend the alien continues to execute its plan for world domination, holding secret meetings with others of its kind and occasionally eating one of the minor characters.

I can really relate to shows like that, because my wife is one of those people. Well, except for the cannibalism part. But she has definitely been showing signs that she is not from around here. This is one of the exciting things about being married to a committed follower of Jesus: they actually change over time. Most people, if you haven't noticed, don't change much, at least not for the better. This is why we categorize people, and feel comfortable leaving them in the same category for years: "He's just naturally grumpy," or "She's a gossip" or "That family has serious issues." If we get to know someone, and then don't see them for several years, when we meet again we will often laugh and say "Same old so-

and-so." Every once in a while, through therapy or a 12-step program or just plain old willpower, people make minor improvements, but for the most part they are who they are. Except for committed Christ-followers. I don't simply say "Christians" because there are plenty of Christians who don't change, other than becoming more and more resistant to change itself. But someone who is really walking with Jesus in close personal relationship will actually be transformed by him. God's Holy Spirit will be inside of them, adding and removing character traits until, in some instances, they become nearly unrecognizable. This is what I am seeing with Carey.

Shortly after I met Carey, I realized that I had to either marry her or spend the rest of my life trying very hard not to think about her. Five years later, I actually did get to marry her, which was much better than trying to forget her, believe me. It's a long story, and probably a lot more interesting to us than it would be to you. The point is that I thought I knew what I was getting into. Carey and I were in love, and we had wonderful dreams of sharing life together. She was a sweet girl, quiet and patient, with impressive character and a deep love for Jesus. She was also, and continues to be, as pretty as a vase of pale blue flowers on a kitchen table in the sunshine. This may be what kept me from guessing her true identity for so long. For the first little while, everything was fine. Then she started reading these books about sharing her faith with her friends and co-workers, which was strange, because she had shown no interest in that subject when we got married. I was going to work in a church, so why did she need to worry about the outside world? I certainly didn't plan on having much contact with the outside world. I planned on surrounding myself with a bunch of friendly church people and having plenty of time left over to write books and climb mountains. Where did this sudden interest in evangelism come from? What was happening to my wife?

Then things got worse. The reading continued. Carey next found some books about heaven, and how it is real and wonderful, and how that should affect the way we spend our time and...our money. Hold on. Now I was getting nervous. Loving Jesus is one thing, and reaching out to the world is okay, but money, as we all know, is a completely separate issue from all that spiritual stuff, especially to someone who is the proud owner of approximately 11 gazillion dollars of student loan debt. She expressed her opinion that we needed to give more to our church, but I pointed out to her that she, unlike her husband, had not priced a good pair of hiking boots lately. Undeterred, she mentioned that it would probably be difficult for me to preach sermons on tithing someday if I didn't do it myself. I responded by explaining that she should shut up now, because I was becoming uncomfortable. This argument somehow failed to convince her. From then on, she began to point out, at very inconvenient times, which things in life were of eternal significance, and which things would not last beyond the "day of the Lord" described in 2 Peter 3:10, when "the heavens will disappear with a roar; the elements will be destroyed by fire, and the earth and everything in it will be laid bare." I began to see the wisdom of the church leaders of the Middle Ages, who felt that it was unnecessary for anybody and everybody to have access to the scriptures. A wife who reads her Bible is a dangerous thing.

I was now thoroughly suspicious. What had happened to the woman I married? Who was this person? Over time, it became harder and harder for her to hide her true nature: she is an alien. Now she talks about heaven as if it were the most normal thing in the world. She draws me into long conversations where we imagine what it will be like. When we go through difficult times, she looks at them from the perspective of our eternal destiny. When we make decisions, she demonstrates eternal values. And then there is the death thing. She honestly isn't afraid of it at all, which is just not human. She says embarrassing things in public about preferring to be with Jesus anyway, away from sin and sorrow and suffering, so hey, the sooner the better, right? If an angel from God were to appear and offer her a choice between going to heaven right now and continuing her work here on earth, it would take her about 10 seconds to decide to leave. If the angel assured her that God said I would be fine, it would take her about 2 seconds. She is a stranger here, and more and more this place is losing its hold on her. It is pretty weird, let me tell you, but I have to admit it's also kind of attractive. I'm starting not to mind having an alien for a wife.

And the thing is, she seems so normal. She likes popcorn and hot chocolate and Disney movies. She talks like a normal person and dresses like a normal person. She works at the mall, for crying out loud. But she can't fool me anymore. I know what's inside. She will be talking with someone about money or some other subject that she finds intensely boring, and she'll be nodding politely and saying "uh-huh," but then her eyes will sort of glaze over and I know exactly where she's going. "I wonder if we will be able to fly in heaven?" she'll be thinking. "I hope so. I wonder if it's true that there's no time there. How will we plan parties?" And the person will be saying, "Blah blah mortgage rates at an all time low blah blah blah," and she'll be saying "Uh-huh. Really?" and at the same time sending up a silent prayer for Jesus to come back before we have to start making house payments. Not that that kind of thing isn't important, just that it isn't eternal or relational. Those things seem to be her main criteria for what matters lately. Like I said, it's pretty weird.

There is an important difference, though, between people like my wife and the aliens on television. The TV aliens always want something; they are consumers who have come for our planet, our bodies, our stuff. Followers of Jesus, on the other hand, have not come to earth because there is something wrong with their home. They would love to be home. They are on Earth because there is something wrong with Earth.

> I eagerly expect and hope that I will in no way be ashamed, but will have sufficient courage so that now as always Christ will be exalted in my body, whether by life or by death. For to me, to live is Christ and to die is gain. If I am to go on

living in the body, this will mean fruitful labor for me. Yet what shall I choose? I do not know! I am torn between the two: I desire to depart and be with Christ, which is better by far; but it is more necessary for you that I remain in the body. Convinced of this, I know that I will remain, and I will continue with all of you for your progress and joy in the faith, so that through my being with you again your joy in Christ Jesus will overflow on account of me (Philippians 1:20-26).

These are the words of Paul, talking about his own life, modeling for us exactly what he meant when he spoke of our heavenly citizenship. He is in prison, awaiting his sentencing, facing the very real possibility that he might die. He firmly believes that Jesus will be exalted, (lifted up for the world to see and worship) either by his life or his death. This is important, because when he says later that he wants to stay alive, we cannot say it is simply "for the glory of God," because he has already made it clear that God is going to be glorified either way. And if it were simply a matter of what would be better for Paul, he would rather die. Don't miss that. In his mind, death is a better option than life. To die is gain. He is so convinced that he will spend eternity with his Savior, and that heaven has infinitely more peace and pleasure to offer than Earth does, that Earth has no hold on him. But there is another factor, something else that overrides these things and makes him want to stick around: the Philippians. Paul's death could glorify God, and it would be a significant improvement for Paul. But the Philippians would miss out on all the encouragement and support they may yet receive from their mentor, pastor, and friend. And so, he makes an incredible statement: I am pretty sure God is going to keep me alive, for your sake. I am on Earth for you.

At some point on the journey toward maturity, every Christian must come to grips with the fact that heaven will be better than this place, yet God is choosing not to take us to heaven yet. Why not? We cannot pretend to fully know God's mind; his reasons are complex, his ways are not our ways. But one reason is clear throughout scripture: God always intended to do more with us than simply save us from death, even spiritual death. His purposes for people are far greater than putting their names on heaven's guest list. He did not send his Son to die because he wanted to increase membership in an organization; he did it to create a family. He did it to make us his children, not only in name but in character. Eventually, he has said that we are to look like Jesus himself. If this is so, if we are to be children of God who look like the Son of God, then we must learn to live for others, and that is a lesson best learned right here on Earth.

The Bible, which Christians say is their authority, contains some words that make some of us uncomfortable. We know that they are in there, but we squirm every time they are mentioned. One of those words is "predestined." Some people feel very strongly about the issue of predestination, so strongly that it is clear they care more about being right and proving others wrong than about demonstrating Christ's love. Personally, I would rather lie on the floor and stare at the ceiling than get into a debate about predestination, but I can't get around the fact that it's in the Bible, so one day I forced myself to sit down and wrestle with exactly what God's Word says about it. I was surprised at what I found. You may be surprised, too. What surprised me was this: all along, I had misunderstood what the Bible says Christians are predestined *for*. If, like me, you have always associated "predestination" with "salvation," read these passages closely:

> Praise be to the God and Father of our Lord Jesus Christ, who has blessed us in the heavenly realms with every spiritual blessing in Christ. For he chose us in him before the creation of the world to be holy and blameless in his sight. In love he *predestined us to be adopted as his sons* through Jesus Christ, in accordance with his pleasure and will—to the praise of his glorious grace, which he has freely given us in the One he loves (Ephesians 1:3-6, italics added).

> And we know that in all things God works for the good of those who love him, who have been called according to his purpose. For those God foreknew he also *predestined to be conformed to the likeness of his son*, that he might be the firstborn among many brothers (Romans 8:28, 29, italics added).

First of all, notice that when the doctrine of predestination appears in scripture, it is meant to be encouraging. Paul offers Christ's followers the concept of predestination as a reason to worship our loving God (Ephesians) and as a comfort in times of trial (Romans). In the years since he wrote, however, the doctrine has been twisted into something else, something that divides the body of Christ into numerous warring factions. Score one for Satan and his crafty little minions. Next, notice why we are supposed to be encouraged: what we are predestined for is not simply salvation, but adoption and sonship. Followers of Jesus are assured that God's plan, from the beginning of time, has been to bring them into his family and then make them look like they belong there. Furthermore, as Paul told the Philippians, he who began a good work in us will carry it on to completion (Php. 1:6). If you are a follower of Jesus, God intends to re-make you into the image of the One you follow, and God always accomplishes what he intends: "What I have said, that will I bring about; what I have planned, that will I do" (Isaiah 46:11). Jesus is our big brother, and we are becoming more like him all the time. We may not always feel it, but it is really happening. It is our destiny.

Admittedly, plenty of Christians leave this earth looking very little like the Son of God. How much of this process is accomplished on earth, and how much in heaven, God only knows. But it is clear that he means to start the process on earth, and that we are called to be active participants in the process, which is mysterious, but not completely unfathomable.

Just as Jesus had to cooperate with his Father's will, while at the same time knowing that it was going to be accomplished without fail, so we must actively seek God's destiny for our lives. As for the bigger question of what it will mean to look like Jesus, books and books and books could be written about the many characteristics of the Son of God we are called to imitate. I am content to focus on one, the one Paul modeled for us: If we are to be like Jesus, we must be selfless.

I do not say this lightly. I am genuinely becoming convinced that selflessness is the main thing, that it is central to understanding and following Christ. From time to time in my ministry, I have come across people who express their discontentedness with shallow Christianity. "We want to go deeper," they say, "We want to be fed. We want to grow." These are good intentions, and I don't mean to be unkind, but whenever I hear this, there is a side of me that wants to ask: "And what do you imagine that will be like?" Sometimes it seems that we have a picture of growth into Christian maturity that is a little too appealing. We imagine ourselves stronger, happier, wiser, and more fulfilled if we could only take our faith to the next level. In some ways, this is true. But in another, more basic way, we have missed what it means to follow Jesus. Following Jesus means, above all, that we stop thinking about ourselves so much. It means denying ourselves and taking up our cross (Matt. 16:24). It means looking not only to our own interests, but also the interests of others (Php. 2:4). It means that, like him, we are servants, living to accomplish the will of the Father and communicate His love to people. That is the destiny God has prepared for us. That is what we are becoming.

By nature, people are self-centered. This was not God's original design for people, but ever since sin entered the world, selfishness has been a character trait shared by every human being to walk the planet. We live for ourselves, and living for ourselves seems so normal that we rarely question it. Our advertising, our economic and governmental systems, even our art and entertainment, all assume that people's lives revolve around themselves, and that this is right and good. We applaud celebrities who give small portions of their huge fortunes to worthy causes and keep the rest for themselves. We blame homelessness on the homeless while supporting an absurdly enormous industry of home-remodeling stores, so that we can make our own houses bigger and fill them with non-necessities. We make our own selfish plans and commitments and then schedule the life of the church into whatever time is left over, and then schedule serving the needy into whatever time is left over after that. Even when we stretch ourselves to our creative limits and try to imagine creatures from another planet, we presume that if there were such creatures, they would be selfish, like us, seeking their own ends above all. We have trouble imagining that there could be another type of being, that life could be oriented toward any other goal.

But what if there were another kind of being? Imagine a Hollywood sci-fi thriller in which one day the sky becomes filled with ominous-looking saucers.

The spacecraft land and are immediately surrounded by military forces. Crowds watch in silence, waiting for the aliens to make their move. Slowly, the door opens and a creature, looking not so very different from us, steps forward. It flicks on its Universal Translator and begins to speak: "Don't mind us; we're just here to help. You people look exhausted and starved for love. Is there anything we can do?" I suppose aliens like that wouldn't make for a very exciting movie. But imagine if it were true: a force of invaders, bent not on taking the world for their own, but on serving its inhabitants. This is what Christians are supposed to be. It is hard for us to remember, and it always has been. Even after spending years with Jesus, the disciples still thought His plan was to beat up the bad guys and take power, and they had their sights set on sharing in that power. Two of them were even brave enough to come right out and ask if they could share the spotlight, and sit on his right and his left when he became king. When the other ten found out about it, they were angry that they hadn't thought of the same thing. This is what Jesus told them:

> You know that those who are regarded as rulers of the Gentiles lord it over them, and their high officials exercise authority over them. Not so with you. Instead, whoever wants to become great among you must be your servant, and whoever wants to be first must be slave of all. For even the Son of Man did not come to be served, but to serve, and to give his life as a ransom for many (Mark 10:42-45).

Christians are supposed to be different. Jesus says to his followers, to you and me, "Everyone around you wants more power, more control over their own lives and other people's lives. Even when they are in a position to help others, they think mostly about themselves. Not so with you. You must be different. You must forget about power, and serve people, thinking about their welfare and not your own, because that is what I do." Jesus, you may remember, is the Son of God. When he says this, he says it as someone who used to live in Heaven—where he had power that would make Donald Trump choke with jealousy—but who has come to Earth for the sake of miserable, sinful human beings. The night before he was crucified, when an armed mob came to arrest him, Jesus restrained his disciples from defending Him. They still did not understand that dying had been his plan all along. If it hadn't been, he certainly wouldn't have needed their help to stay alive. "Do you think I cannot call on my Father, and he will at once put at my disposal more than twelve legions of angels?" he asked (Matt. 26:53). He knew more about power than they ever would. He also knew that, when it came to the Father's purposes for humanity, power was not the point. Love was the point. Love leads us to put others first, to serve them. And so he called his followers to this incredible task: Give your lives away, as I have, for the sake of others.

> Do nothing out of selfish ambition or vain conceit, but in humility consider others better than yourselves. Each of you should look not

only to his own interests, but also to the interests of others. Your attitude should be the same as that of Christ Jesus, who, being in very nature God, did not consider equality with God something to be grasped, but made himself nothing, taking the very nature of a servant, being made in human likeness (Php. 2: 3-7).

When I was a teenager, the word "radical" was very popular. Today it has been replaced by much better words, like "phat" and "dope." Back in the late 80's no one wanted to be called a fat dope, but to be called "radical," or simply "rad," was definitely a compliment. If someone or something was radical, it meant that they were fresh and new, not afraid to be completely different from what was normal. My youth pastor caught on to this, and began challenging us to be "radical" in our Christianity. To be a radical Christian meant that we were sold out to Jesus, that God had control of our entire lives, not just certain safe parts of them. It meant that we were not afraid to be completely different from the people around us. He even suggested that biblically there really was no other way to live the Christian life. We knew he was taking things a little too far; you only had to look at the adults in our church to see that it was perfectly possible to be a Christian without getting so carried away. But it was an interesting thought.

Then again, what Paul said to the Philippians was pretty radical: Do nothing out of selfish ambition or vain conceit. Don't do anything out of self-interest. If we assume that what he meant by this was that followers of Jesus really aren't supposed to do anything out of pride or a desire for selfish gain, then it becomes clear that the Philippians were going to have to be radically different from everyone around them. They were going to have to re-orient their lives, away from themselves and toward God and others. They were going to have to get out of bed in the morning with the attitude that God had left them on this planet to benefit someone else, the same attitude Paul had already demonstrated toward them. It would be hard, because it would go against their own human nature and everything they were learning from the culture around them. But it would be the only way they could really claim to be followers of Jesus.

And so this is what Christians are supposed to be: an army of invaders, bent on merciful service to the dying world around them. Like Jesus, we are sent to this planet, away from the home we love, to convince people of the compassion of our Heavenly Father, and invite them to join us on the return journey. We are called to enter our cities, our jobs, our schools, our churches, and our world as He did, not to be served but to serve. We are given bodies that look like those around us, so that we can move in and out of society and implement our strategies of grace. These bodies hide our true identity as citizens of a distant land, aliens on earth. Our mission is not quickly accomplished, and we face the very real danger of forgetting who we are and why we have come. If we lose our focus on heaven, we begin to think that perhaps we are here for our own good, and we look to this place to satisfy the desires of our soul. Soon, we are consumed with our own needs and wants, and forget about those we are here to love.

Focus came more easily for Jesus. In his sinless perfection he was far less forgetful than you and me. The Bible says that he endured the agony of the cross, bearing the sin of the world and its consequences—death and separation from His Father—for a very specific reason: "the joy set before him" (Heb. 12:2). In other words, he knew that it would be worth it. Sharing eternity with all of us, sitting down at his Father's right hand after accomplishing his will, having defeated death and hell, would be better, more joyful, than simply letting us die and keeping heaven to himself. This goal, the joy of heaven, kept him going through the pain of Calvary. It is the same with us. We give our lives away on earth because we are storing up treasures in heaven, and then going there to enjoy them.

Of course, all of this sounds very noble until you go out and try to serve some real live people. People can be jerks. Not always, but enough that it makes it hard to give your life away to them. This is why good theology, believe it or not, is actually pretty important. If you don't understand that what you are really doing is worshiping God, then serving people will burn you out in a hurry. I used to work closely with some people who had given themselves to serving the poor in inner-city Denver. One time I asked them how they found the strength to keep going. Without hesitation, they said that they had to be constantly reminded that what they did, they did for Jesus. "If you take the attitude that you're doing this just because you love people, you'll discover how unloving you really are in about six weeks," one of them said. "People are ungrateful sinners. We do what we do because Jesus did it, and we are following Him."

I imagine that the Philippians were not much different from the people on the streets of Denver: human, and sinful, and needy. But Paul, for Jesus' sake, was willing to make them his reason for living. He described the big dreams he had for them, that they would grow in their faith and become beacons of God's love for the world to see, messengers of His Word. If they did this, it would mean "that I may boast on the day of Christ that I did not run or labor for nothing" (Php. 2:16). Paul actually planned to invite God to evaluate his life based on the transformed lives of the people he encountered. He said something similar to another group, the Thessalonians: "For what is our hope, our joy, or the crown in which we will glory in the presence of our Lord Jesus when he comes. Is it not you? Indeed, you are our glory and joy" (1 Thess. 2:19). When Jesus asked him what he had done with his life, Paul would simply point to the Thessalonians, with tears of joy running down his face. Later, he told them that he found happiness in a prison cell when he learned of their spiritual progress:

> Therefore, brothers, in all our distress and persecution we were encouraged about you because of your faith. For now we really live, since you are

standing firm in the Lord. How can we thank God enough for you in return for all the joy we have in the presence of God because of you? Night and day we pray most earnestly that we may see you again and supply what is lacking in your faith (1 Thess. 3:7-10).

I don't know about you, but I'm a little jealous of the Thessalonians and the Philippians. If I am honest, something deep in my soul desperately wants someone to feel about me the way Paul felt about these people. I imagine that it must have been very easy, very natural, for them to believe in a heavenly Father who is loving and gracious and kind. They probably thought he was a little like Paul: concerned for their welfare, looking out for their interests, even at great cost to himself. For millions today, it is much harder to imagine such a Father. We live in a world full of people who have never had someone look them in the eye and say "You are my glory and my joy." That kind of love is foreign, alien, to them. And that kind of love is our task on this earth. It is why we are here.

Chapter Three

the church: aliens unanimous

Paul was not the only early Christian who understood that we don't really belong here. Peter, who was one of Jesus' closest companions, became strongly convinced that followers of Jesus shouldn't make the mistake of getting too comfortable here on Earth. He didn't start out that way, of course. He started out as a fisherman, making a living with his hands. Smelly fish, tired muscles, long hours, and poor wages were the realities of his early years; like most people, he spent most of his time thinking about the only world he knew, the one he saw around him when he woke up in the morning. Then he met Jesus. After three years of listening to Jesus' teaching, watching his life, death, and resurrection, and then being filled with God's Holy Spirit and leading the church during its first crucial steps, Peter had a new perspective on this world. This is why, when he was writing a letter to his fellow Christians, he addressed it "To God's elect, strangers in the world" (1 Peter 1:1).

I know the word "elect," like "predestined," triggers strong feelings among some Christians. Thankfully, including it in Scripture was not my idea; it was God's. If it bothers you, I'll let you take it up with him. It is not really what this book is about anyway. For our purposes, it simply means that if one day you wake up and discover that you're a follower of Jesus, don't congratulate yourself too much. People don't get the credit for choosing God; God chooses us. It is an awesome privilege and a deep mystery, and, sadly, the starting point for numerous heated arguments between God's people. These arguments, along with a lot of other things, will all be sorted out one day when we stand sheepishly before the throne of the One who made everything from nothing so that he could share eternal life with us.

What is important here is that Peter also calls Christians "strangers in the world." That is how he thinks of us, and of himself. He doesn't go into a long explanation to help us understand that we are strangers; he assumes that we are, and that we know it. A little later, he says it again: "Since you call on a Father who judges each man's work impartially, live your lives as strangers here in reverent fear" (1:17). Then he says it a third time: "Dear friends, I urge you, as aliens and strangers in the world, to abstain from sinful desires, which war against your soul" (2:11). In other words, since you have a relationship with the living God of the universe, who created you and will one day take you home, live to meet his standards, not those of the world in which you find yourself. That world is temporary. Furthermore, the body you inhabit, which still tends to want things that are against God's will, is also temporary. Don't live to satisfy its desires; live to take good care of your eternal soul.

Most Christians know that they are supposed to please God and flee from sin. But not many of us, when we were taught these things, were given this reason: you are strangers and aliens on earth, so start acting like it. But that is what Peter says. Just today, Carey and I spent an hour and a half in "Children's Church" with a roomful of 3-year-olds while their parents worshiped upstairs. It was loads of fun. We sang songs and learned about Noah's ark and talked about obeying God. Then we made our own animal masks and pretended we were on the ark, and then we ate lots and lots of marshmallows. I think the marshmallows were actually supposed to be glued to something as part of an art project of some kind, but mostly we ate them. One thing we did not do, though, is explain to the kids that if they love God and want to obey him like Noah, they had better plan on being freaks and outcasts for the rest of their lives. I guess they were probably too young for that, but then I have to wonder, at what age do we break it to them? I think if Peter volunteered in Children's Church, he would make sure that, at some point, all the little prospective Christians would be given the "strangers and aliens" talk. Then they could go home and talk to their parents about it. "What did you learn at church today?" the parents would ask. "That I'm a alien, and I'll never be cool," the little child would reply. And the proud parents would say, "Thank God for those wonderful volunteers in Children's Church!" At least, that's how I picture it.

I was a youth pastor once, but not for very long. I was terrible at it. I think the basic problem was that a lot of youth ministry has to do with having a good time, which has never been a real strength of mine. The teens would ask, "What are we going to do this summer, Brian?" And I'd say, "What do you mean, what are we going to do? This is church; we're going to study the Bible." Then they'd get this look on their face like someone had just handed them a plate full of brussel sprouts. Since then, I have learned that few people, and even fewer 14-year-olds, like to sit around and study the Bible as much as I do. But even when we weren't studying the Bible, I wasn't much of a youth pastor. A lot of youth pastors do a great job of making Christianity appealing, and of drawing young people into the kingdom of God through a combination of patience, love, giftedness, and trendy hairstyles. I admire them, but I am not one of them. My basic philosophy as a youth pastor was that you cannot wholeheartedly follow Jesus without letting go of some of the things our culture values most. Pursue Christ, and you can kiss your dreams of popularity goodbye. For some reason, my youth ministry did not experience significant growth. Perhaps I was a little misguided, but I still think the basic principle is true: if you call yourself a follower of Christ, then you are a stranger, an alien. Start acting like it.

I think it is safe to say that most of the world knows that Christians are supposed to live differently from everyone else. Sometimes we do a good job of being different; sometimes we just talk about it. Unfortunately, the world often thinks exclusively in terms of the things we *don't* do. Later in this book we'll address some of the things that Christians say no to while the world says yes. Self-denial is an important part of following Christ, but I don't believe it's the best place to start. The most exciting part of our heavenly citizenship is all of the things we get to enjoy that everyone else is missing out on. And one of those things, believe it or not, is something most of us do all the time, without realizing what a special privilege it is. One of the best things about being a Christian, to my mind, is the weekly opportunity to gather with other believers in worship. We get to go to church.

Every Sunday morning, millions of people all across the country do something that makes absolutely no sense to their friends, family, and neighbors. While everyone else is sleeping in or getting some work done around the house, going boating or hiking or surfing, sleeping off hangovers or getting ready to watch football, Christians go to church. Why do we do this? Some of us go because we are part of really fun cutting-edge churches, where the music is catchy and inspiring and the teaching is hip and relevant, but also biblical and life-transforming. I know this because I have read books about such places, and they sound great. But statistics show that most of us do not worship in that kind of church. Most of us go to churches that are small to medium-sized. Our music is several years (or decades) behind anything our unchurched friends would voluntarily sing along with. Our sermons often contain truth, but truth that can seem distant from the realities of our lives. And yet we continue to show up there, week after week. Why? What is the big deal about going to church?

I was thinking about this the other day at the gym, when I struck up a conversation between sets with an older guy I had seen there before. He came over and started giving me all these pointers on how to lift more weight without hurting myself, and it was clear that he knew his stuff. He was one of these guys who are so naturally athletic that it never occurs to them that many people devote their lives to something other than having fun with their bodies. He was in his late 50's or early 60's, his kids were grown, he had money to burn, and he was into everything you could think of. He was a skier and a snowboarder and a water-skier and a wind-surfer and a deep-sea fisherman and a big-game hunter and probably a hang-glider and a skydiver. His latest interest was kiteboarding, which, if you're not familiar with it, is basically a cross between surfing and strapping yourself to a rocket. He had all sorts of great stories about the various injuries and surgeries he had undergone in his relentless pursuit of the next rush. He was the kind of person that has spawned an entire industry of stores, magazines, outfitters, and resorts in our culture. He was someone who worked hard and played even harder. And he made it all sound like so much fun, even the painful parts. In my mind, I began referring to him as The Man Who Never Grew Up.

And here is my confession: standing there listening to The Man Who Never Grew Up, I discovered a deep jealousy welling up from somewhere within me. In that moment, I realized that a part of me wanted very much to trade places with this guy who had devoted his life to having fun. I also realized that part of the reason he had been able to do all of those things was that, for him, Sunday was just another Saturday. Having gone to church my whole life, I have had comparatively few opportunities to take two days in a row and do whatever I want with them. I started thinking about how I had just spent the last 3 years in Colorado, and ended up leaving without climbing a lot of the mountains I had hoped to climb. You can climb a lot more mountains in two days a week than you can in one, but when you are on staff at a church, you usually get one, and sometimes not even that. I remembered Sunday mornings in college, standing outside the dorm waiting for a ride to church while the rest of the campus was still recovering from the night before. If you are ever on a typical college campus early on a Sunday morning, you might very well catch yourself imagining that you are the sole survivor of a nuclear holocaust. It is a lonely feeling. And just for a moment, there in the gym with The Man Who Never Grew Up, I began to wonder if it had all been worth it.

The moment of weakness passed, of course. God soon reminded me of the life that I find only in him, now and for eternity, which is the greatest privilege and source of joy I can imagine, and which I would not really trade for anything. But it did make me think that perhaps we could all use a reminder of why we go to church. For a long time, I thought Christians went to church because if we didn't, God would be mad. I thought we went as some sort of payment to God, as if we were earning points with God whenever we walked through the front doors of the church building. Many Christians, I think, live with this sort of inner conflict. Theologically, we know that God loves us unconditionally, and saves us by his grace alone. Practically, though, we do a lot of things solely because we are afraid of what will happen if we don't. Now, it is a noble thing to do something out of a sense of duty. But because we are weak and sinful humans, duty will only keep us going for so long. And there are much, much better reasons to go to church:

> Therefore, brothers, since we have confidence to enter the Most Holy Place by the blood of Jesus, by a new and living way opened for us through the curtain, that is, his body, and since we have a great high priest over the house of God, let us draw near to God with a sincere heart in full assurance of faith, having our hearts sprinkled to cleanse us from a guilty conscience and having our bodies washed with pure water. Let us hold unswervingly to the hope we profess, for he who promised is faithful. And let us consider how we may spur one another on toward love and good deeds. Let us not give up meeting together, as

some are in the habit of doing, but let us encourage one another—and all the more as you see the Day approaching (Hebrews 10:19-25).

The writer of Hebrews assumes a lot here. He knew his readers were Jewish, and thus completely familiar with the system of worship outlined in the Old Testament. He also hoped that they had been paying attention to everything he had written leading up to chapter 10. For those of us who are neither Jewish nor familiar with Hebrews chapters 1-9, let me summarize: In the old system, God was inaccessible. The temple, where worship took place, provided a visual reminder of the walls between people and God. The Most Holy Place, where God's presence dwelt in a unique way the Bible doesn't fully explain, was off limits to everyone except a specially selected priest, who entered once a year to offer sacrifice for the sins of the people. But now, the writer of Hebrews says that anyone, everyone, can enter God's presence, and enter it with confidence. Jesus' body and blood, given for our sins, can make us clean and remove the curtain between us and God. Jesus now serves as our priest, the only priest we need, so that we don't need a go-between; we can approach God directly. This, in fact, is exactly what God and the author of Hebrews want us to do: "Let us draw near to God."

An entire book could be written about the privilege Christians have of drawing near to God—not just receiving a ticket into heaven, but actually experiencing intimacy with the awesome Being who made them from nothing. In fact, there are many such books, and they are worth finding and reading. But for the purposes of this book, simply notice who the author is writing to. Who has confidence to enter the Most Holy Place? Who has a great high priest? We do. Who draws near to God and has their hearts sprinkled and all the rest? Us. The words "we" and "us" are repeated throughout the passage. Not just you, or just me. You and me and everybody, all together. This passage is painting a picture of the Christian life, and intimacy with God is only half of the picture. The other half is intimacy with people. We draw near to God together.

As Americans, we value independence, and it's hard for most of us to grasp that God simply doesn't share our values. He is not impressed with people who go it alone—quite the opposite, in fact. While we celebrate self-sufficiency, God's heart is breaking over our self-centeredness. We have even come to interpret the Bible individualistically, but that is a mistake. Most of the Bible was not written to individuals, but to groups. When the New Testament uses the word "you," in the original Greek it is usually you plural—a more literal translation, as much as it pains an English major like me to say it, would be "y'all." This passage, then, with its repetition of "let us," is giving Jesus' followers, *as a group,* some instructions on how to live, now that there is no barrier between them and their God. Here is what they, and we, are encouraged to do together:

1) First, as we have seen, it says "Let us draw near to God." God really is saying, "Don't feel like you have to keep your distance; get up close to me.

It's what Jesus died for." And he is clearly saying that we are to do this as a group. We don't just draw near to God when we are alone in private times of prayer, although that is important. It is also supposed to happen when we gather with other followers of Jesus.

2) Next, "Let us hold unswervingly to the hope we profess, for he who promised is faithful." Together, even though it is hard, we are told to hang on to the hope of eternal life. God will not let us down; we can count on heaven. Somehow, Christians must find a way to help each other keep eternity in view.

3) Then, "Let us consider how we may spur one another on toward love and good deeds." Be thinking, God says, about how you can help your fellow Christians live out their faith by showing Jesus' love to the world. Christ's followers need to remind and encourage each other to live like him.

4) Finally, "And let us not give up meeting together, as some are in the habit of doing, but let us encourage each other—and all the more as you see the Day approaching." In this statement, the author shares the secret of how we can do everything he is calling us to do. The way to draw near to God, hold onto our hope, and encourage one another in living a life of love is simple: Christians must meet together often. We need each other desperately. Apparently, even in the first century, some people were already giving up on the whole church thing. They had their relationship with Jesus; they were going to heaven, but getting together with other believers, for whatever reason, didn't seem like a good use of their

time. Many Christians today feel the same way. Ironically, they forget that heaven itself is going to consist largely of relationships—with God and with others. Those people we are avoiding at church are our brothers and sisters for all of eternity; we might as well start learning to get along.

It's also worth noticing that all of this is related to "the Day." Christians are to come together to encourage one another "all the more as you see the Day approaching." A day is coming when Jesus will return, to judge the earth and take God's children home to heaven. As that day approaches, we will need each other all the more, because being a follower of Jesus is not going to get any easier between now and then. One of the important functions of God's church, though certainly not the only one, is that of a haven or retreat, because the reality is that Christians are different from the rest of the world. Monday through Saturday, we are surrounded by people who are not living in anticipation of Christ's return. When we gather for worship, we open our hearts to express our love to the One who is coming back to take us home, and to hear His Word to us, in the company of other people who are doing the same thing. It is tremendously refreshing. Together, we seek the presence of God here on earth, because together we are all waiting until we can be in his presence for eternity. Of course, in some churches it is hard to tell that this is why people are gathered, but biblically, this is the goal.

Some of us may struggle to embrace this view of church because we are the products of a consumer culture. We are used to thinking of church as a place we drive to, an event we attend, where the people on stage have the responsibility of singing and preaching and doing other things to help us feel near to God. We speak of "going to church," because we "go to" movies and baseball games and the mall. But the Bible never speaks of going to church. Biblically, church is not an event we attend; it is something we are a part of. It is not entertainment, it is a community. This means, among other things, that we must be careful of the way we approach the process of "shopping" for a church. Are we looking for a show that we enjoy, for services and programs that meet our expectations, or for a group of Christ-followers to join? Sometimes we say that we care so much about what happens on stage because we are looking for a "worshipful environment." Lately, though, I have to admit that I'm not so sure a worshipful environment is created by the few people on the stage for the benefit of the rest of us. Maybe a church service feels more "worshipful" when more people enter into it with the attitude that they are participants, not spectators, gathered for the purpose of drawing near to God.

All of this will make perfect sense to you if you are familiar with the concept of a support group. Many people outside of Christianity have learned the value of being around people who are going through the same thing they are. If you have a disease or an addiction or a tragedy in your family, you can find support in a group of people who sympathize, who offer you advice and encouragement and friendship based on their own similar experiences. These groups become like families because they understand each other's struggles. This is one of the functions of the church: it acts as a support group for followers of Jesus, people whose citizenship is in heaven and who find themselves greatly misunderstood by the world around them. Personally, I think a great name for a church would be Aliens Unanimous—"anonymous" wouldn't work, since Jesus' followers are not ashamed of the One they follow. I am considering proposing this name for the church where I am a new staff member. I'll let you know how that goes.

My wife, as I have mentioned, like's children's movies. Making me watch them with her is her subtle way of reminding me that we really do need to have kids someday. The other day we curled up on the couch and gave two hours of our lives to the movie *Muppets from Space*. I had pretty much written the evening off as one of those sacrifices you make because you're married. I found, instead, that the writers of this little film actually understood something pretty central to the human experience: the need to belong. The central character in the story is Gonzo, a cute little muppet whose genus and species are something of a mystery. Gonzo lives with a bunch of frogs and pigs and bears and chickens and rats, all of whom find their identity in the fact that everywhere they look, they see other creatures like themselves. They know who they are and where they belong. But who, or what, is Gonzo? He becomes so discouraged by his isolation that he convinces himself he is receiving messages from space, sent by other creatures like him. Despite the taunts of his friends and neighbors, he clings to the belief that he is not alone. His hope leads him to do some crazy things, and he becomes increasingly misunderstood. His friends think he is obsessed with a silly dream, but he doesn't care; he is desperate to believe that there are others like him. Then Hollywood takes over, and everything falls apart: the other aliens actually show up, but Gonzo decides to stay on earth with the pigs and rats, and there is a big musical number. The comparison to Christianity kind of breaks down at that point, but you get the idea. Nobody likes to be alone. And yet many followers of Jesus are trying to live the Christian life in a terribly lonely fashion, clinging to the hope of a heavenly home without the support and encouragement of their fellow heavenly citizens.

Peter, the same guy who called Christians "strangers and aliens" in 1 Peter 2:11, called us some other names in that same passage of scripture, which, if we understood them, are probably even more shocking:

> But you are a chosen people, a royal priesthood, a holy nation, a people belonging to God, that you may declare the praises of him who called you out of darkness into his wonderful light. Once you were not a people, but now you are the people of God; once you had not received mercy, but now you have received mercy (1 Peter 2:9,10).

Again, remember where Peter got his start: untangling nets down at the dock. And now listen to him as he tries to help his fellow Christ-followers grasp their true identity. This is what Jesus does to a person, to Peter and to Peter's friends and to you and me. Once we were so lost and deceived we actually thought that earth was our home, and we certainly had no significant connection to the people around us. But now, we are a part of a group that has been selected, chosen by God, to receive his great mercy and then praise him for it in front of the entire world. He calls us a "royal priesthood." Stop and think about some of the people you see at church, who are at times all too human. Is there anything royal or priestly about them? Maybe not on the outside. But if they are believers in Jesus, that is their true identity. They belong to a "holy nation," a spiritual race of people who have been cleansed in God's sight and brought into right relationship with him. You do not go to church with ordinary people. You go to church with the chosen few, royal priests, holy people who have been brought out of the darkness and into the light. And you are one of them. You, too, if you are a Christian, are one of these "saints," as Paul called us (Philippians 1:1). You are, in God's sight, drastically different from the world around you. This is why you need other Christians. Without the companionship of your fellow aliens, you will always be alone and misunderstood, a lonely Gonzo in a world of pigs and rats.

Hopefully, all of this gives new perspective to the whole question of giving up our weekends. God's church is something we cannot do without. It is what prepares and preserves us for heaven. It is also, by the way, a temporary arrangement. When we all get to heaven, we will not be aliens anymore. We won't need a church, because all of heaven will be the church. We won't need reminders to hang in there or to be good. We will have arrived at our destination in every way, perfected people living in a perfect place. And we won't have to set aside time for drawing near to God, because time will no longer matter, and God will always be near. We will be near to him when we are gathered to sing songs, or when we are climbing mountains (which I personally believe will be bigger, and more beautiful, than the ones in Colorado that I never got to climb). And it will be clear to us then that it was the people who missed out on church, and not us, who were wasting their time on Sunday mornings.

Chapter Four

you and your planet: vessels in need of repair

When Carey and I first moved to town, we told our hosts that we didn't know how long it would be until we could find a house, but we hoped no more than a few weeks. Because that is what we believed, we didn't really make any effort to get settled in our new surroundings. We left our clothes in suitcases and ate a lot of fast food. There's no point in getting too comfortable when you'll be moving on in a matter of days.

That was three months ago. When we decided to buy the house on Neptune, which at that point existed only on paper, everything changed. Building a house on the Oregon coast is like eating at The Olive Garden on a Saturday night: if you want it fast, you should've gone somewhere else. Once we came to grips with the fact that our temporary situation was not going to be so temporary after all, we started doing things differently. We unpacked our clothes and bought groceries. We became more conscientious about contributing to household chores. We brought home a carload of necessities from our storage unit, Carey got a job, and we did our best to find a routine. Every day now, we get up in this strange house and go off to work, where we interact with people who assume that, like them, we are waiting for the end of the day, when we can go home and relax. But we are different from them. We have no home. We are waiting for a day many months from now, when we can go home and relax. We are getting by, making do. It is a strange way to live. We feel that things will be so much better when our house is finished, and yet we believe that God is sovereign, and that he is doing important things, in us and through us, in this time of waiting. We are trying our best to submit ourselves to His plan, which we know in our heads is the best plan. Every once in a while, though, it all feels like too much. One of us will return from a long day, flop down on the bed in the small spare room that has become the center of our temporary universe, and say "I just want to go home."

This is not to say anything bad about our hosts, or the house they are so generously sharing with us. They are great people, and they have bent over backwards to make room for us, from sharing space in their refrigerator to putting up with Sugar, our adorable, energetic, obnoxious little dog. Their house is great, too. It is in a beautiful spot, and has plenty of room for all of us. The only problem is that it isn't ours. It is hard to describe the way we feel. If you have ever been sick when you were on vacation, when not being in your own bed makes everything seem ten times worse, or if you've been in an overcrowded house for the holidays and found yourself secretly wanting to get away from all the friends and family for a few minutes, even though you love them, then you have some idea of what we are going through. We are simply not at home, and it is tiring. And yet, for now, it's all we have, and so we are making the best of it, working hard at our jobs and trying to remember to pull our weight and load the dishwasher once in a while, even though we often feel like hiding under the covers until moving day.

This extended detour certainly wasn't part of our plan when we left Colorado last summer. But it doesn't surprise me. I know why it is happening. A couple of times in my life, I have made the mistake of telling Jesus that I want to be more like him. I have invited the Father to shape my heart, my character, so that I resemble his Son. I don't know what I was thinking, but it's too late to take it back now. Carey has done the same thing. And so God is doing this because He is answering our prayers. He is showing us what it means to be like Jesus in this world.

> As they were walking along the road, a man said to him, "I will follow you wherever you go." Jesus replied, "Foxes have holes and birds of the air have nests, but the Son of Man has no place to lay his head" (Luke 9: 57,58).

Jesus was in this world for thirty-three years, but he didn't ever really get comfortable here. It was never home for him. He made sure people knew that following him meant being on a journey, relinquishing the comforts of home to set out on a great quest. I am slowly, often reluctantly, coming to terms with the fact that in order to truly call myself his disciple I must release my desperate grasp on this world. What is hard about that, of course, is that I am still in this world. It may not be home, but it is all I have ever known. So what exactly am I supposed to do with this place? This is not a new question, of course. Christians have always struggled with knowing how to view this life, this temporary situation that is not so temporary. For the first few decades after Jesus ascended into heaven, many were convinced that his return would come soon, within a few months or years. If this was the case, there was no need to put much effort into worldly pursuits. In fact, it got to the point that Paul actually had to instruct his beloved Thessalonians to go out and get jobs. In his first letter to them, he encouraged them with the promise of the Lord's coming, but in his second letter, he was compelled to plead with them to avoid idleness and not be a burden to others: "If a man will not work, he shall not eat" (2 Thess. 3:10). Yes, Jesus is coming back soon. No, you can't just lie around and stare up at the sky and mooch off your parents.

Today, however, Christians have a different struggle (although we are still producing our share of people who mooch off their parents). Jesus did not return right away, and so his followers have unpacked their suitcases. In today's Christianity, at least in America, we are in very little danger of being so distracted by Jesus' certain return that we fail to take care of everyday responsibilities. Instead, we run the risk of having such high hopes for this world, for the achievements and pleasures and false securities it can offer, that we forget to think about his return at all. If the Thessalonians had their heads in the clouds, ours are in the sand. We have ceased to dream of heaven, and are trying desperately to fulfill our dreams on earth.

I first began dreaming of heaven on my honeymoon in Hawaii. I was working as a youth pastor in the Portland area when Carey and I got married, and it was the middle of a rainy Oregon winter, so stealing away to a sunny beach somewhere was pretty appealing. Some people think pastors shouldn't take honeymoons in Hawaii, because it is too self-indulgent, but at the time I was unaware of this. All I knew was that I was in my first salaried job ever, and my bride wanted to go to Hawaii, and I felt like husband of the year because I was going to take her there. I didn't actually have the money for it, so I put it on my credit card. I figured that people with salaries can pay off their credit cards, which was a great theory, except that after a year I resigned my position because, as I mentioned before, I turned out to be a terrible youth pastor. Subsequent jobs didn't pay quite so well, so five years later I am actually still paying for the trip to Hawaii. Some people think this is bad, too, because Christians shouldn't have credit card debt. These are people who like to use the word "prudent" a lot, and who make you feel like you are wasting God's money when you don't buy generic orange juice. In general, I agree with them, except that love isn't always prudent. Carey happens to be picky about her orange juice, and she is my princess. My love for her cannot always be restrained by realities as mundane as the checkbook. I would grow my own oranges and squeeze them for her every morning, if I had the time and skill and lived somewhere a little sunnier. Since I couldn't do that, I figured I could at least give her a good honeymoon. And she loved Hawaii. We both did, actually. We had an absolute blast, and I was husband of the year, and we still talk about it all the time. Our marriage began with the foundation of those shared experiences, those extravagant moments of celebration. We have never regretted it, except when explaining it to people who didn't think it was prudent.

Anyway, Hawaii is where I really started to long for heaven. And not for the reasons you might expect: it wasn't that Hawaii was "a little slice of heaven" or anything like that—just the opposite, in fact. Supposedly, Hawaii is an example of the best this world has to offer, and yet I discovered that I was secretly disappointed by it. Underneath all the fun I was having, I began to feel a ripple of discontentment within myself that I didn't talk about at first, because I was embarrassed. Somehow, I wanted more, but I felt guilty about it. It was a feeling I had not expected. I had expected paradise, but I began to suspect that perhaps I was looking for paradise in the wrong place, that maybe the whole world was looking in the wrong place, because the world is the wrong place to look. This idea made me a little uncomfortable, so I did my best to shove the feeling aside and just enjoy myself. Most of the time, this was fairly easy. Each day was rich with joy and pleasure. We hiked in the rain through tropical forests and along wild coastline. We kayaked in the rivers and swam in the waterfalls and snorkeled with the dazzling fish, and laughed at the thought of the people back home in the cold, gray winter. We also did all of the other stuff you would expect a couple to do on their honeymoon, which is really none of your business, although I will say it beat snorkeling by a long shot. Still, at the end of the day, no matter what we had done, I would lie in bed as Carey drifted off to sleep and try to make sense of this lack of peace, this restlessness I could not ignore.

It is hard to explain exactly why I wasn't satisfied, why, on a Hawaiian honeymoon, I could still sense a hunger somewhere deep in my soul. Some people would say that I want too much, that if a week in an island paradise with a beautiful new bride doesn't satisfy me, nothing will. This is what I thought, at first. I would watch the sun set over the ocean, hear the wind in the palm trees, put my arm around Carey, and try to convince myself that I was perfectly happy, perfectly at peace, because it would be foolish to be anything else. But perfection was still out of reach. The beautiful things and beautiful experiences failed to accomplish something within me, to provide something that I had always assumed the world could provide, if only I was patient enough. My illusions were stripped away, which I am learning is actually a good thing, although it is painful at first. When you lose your illusions, reality becomes clearer. I began to see Hawaii through the lenses of reality, and I was surprised at what I saw.

There was, first of all, the fact that I couldn't really afford to be there, putting me in a category with most of the rest of the earth's population. Everything there was pretty expensive. Native Hawaiians can't even afford to live by the ocean anymore; the tourist industry has driven them inland to the less valuable property no one else wants. And the more desirable the location, the worse it gets. I recently read about another tropical getaway, the Seychelles Islands in the Indian Ocean. The first European explorer to visit there called the islands "the original Garden of Eden." The magazine writer actually claimed to have found paradise. This was his description: "With lush mountain peaks, brilliant white beaches, and rare creatures like the Aldabra giant tortoise, the islands remain a place where disease is virtually unknown, crime is almost non-existent, and pollution—what pollution?" He recommended a particular resort on the islands, "where world-class diving and snorkeling are just a short walk from your private luxury villa." Sounded good to me. Then I read the cost: $1639 per person, per day. If Carey and I had gone there for 7 days, the cost of our honeymoon would have been $22,946, or roughly the cost of a new car, or a year's worth of college tuition, or more than someone growing up in Haiti will earn in a lifetime of hard labor.

So paradise is for rich people. That hardly seems fair. On top of this, I noticed that there were a whole lot of people working their tails off to support my 7 days in paradise. Hotel clerks, waiters, the lady behind the counter at the grocery store, flight attendants, and the guy who hoses down the kayaks when you're done with them all had one thing in common: they were not on vacation. They were working, usually for a few bucks an hour, so that I could play. And I could only play for a few days; then I would have to go back to work. It seemed that the whole world was working so that a few people at a time could take a little break. Some people work their whole lives, often at jobs they do not love, so that they can afford to buy a motor home and drive around enjoying a couple of years of peace, quiet, and scenic beauty before their bodies fall apart and they die. While they are driving around, they expect that other people will be hard at work at gas stations and restaurants and RV parks so that they can have their fun. In this way, we are all basically in competition with one another to carve out for ourselves a little heaven on earth. My paradise depends on your labor. Even in the Seychelles, someone has to clean the toilets.

Not only is paradise for rich people, then, but it depends on poor people to keep it running and provide leisure for the select few. Ugh. The more I saw the way things really work, the more I started to feel like it was okay to want more than Hawaii can offer. It seemed that no matter what incredible experience the world offered me, something about it was tainted, and temporary. I have a friend, a social worker, who spent 6 weeks in Hawaii working with low-income native families. She never wants to go back. The poverty, the drug use, the hopelessness, and the deep resentment toward outsiders were more than she could take. At first, when she described her experience, I realized that part of me didn't want to hear it, because I didn't want it to be true. But I knew that it was. Hawaii, for all its beauty, is not heaven.

I had a similar experience when I lived in Colorado. I have always loved mountains. I love climbing them, looking at them, being near them. At one point in my life, I had the opportunity to study at an excellent seminary in the Chicago area, and I ended up leaving after only one semester, largely because I was lonely for mountains. Something about the beauty and challenge they provide, and the fact that I grew up around them, makes mountains my favorite part of creation. And yet mountains are not heaven either. On numerous occasions, driving along the Front Range of the Colorado Rockies, staring up at the peaks, picking out the few I had climbed from the many I hadn't, I was overcome with what I can only describe as a mixture of awe and frustration. I realized, in those moments, that climbing the mountains wasn't what I really wanted most. When I looked at them, a deep desire was awakened within me that wasn't satisfied even when I walked among them and stood on top of them. I wanted something more, to possess them almost, to take what they represented and somehow put it inside myself. The truth is, I didn't know what I wanted to do with them; I only knew that they made me aware of a need that

I couldn't meet, and that they couldn't meet. They made me homesick, but they were not home.

Another thing about mountains: like an island paradise, they are not accessible to everyone. Many people don't have bodies healthy enough to explore the great outdoors, or checkbooks healthy enough to drop hundreds of dollars obtaining all the latest gear. Even those who do have these things, for the most part, also have jobs, and so they can only hope for a little taste of paradise as their work schedule permits. On a Saturday morning in Colorado, you can get up at 3 in the morning and drive several hours into the mountains to some remote trailhead, and there will be 200 cars in the parking lot. People talk about what a great thing that is, how Coloradoans have such an "active lifestyle." This is somewhat true, but my impression is that it's also a desperate lifestyle, cramming every possible moment with the pursuit of satisfaction. And this pursuit, once again, is reserved for people of privilege. When I interacted with the people who live on the streets of Denver, I noticed that they rarely looked at the mountains, which were quite nearby. They were focused on their next meal, and on staying warm that night. They needed hats and gloves, but not for skiing or hiking. They had plenty of free time, but sleeping on the concrete left them without any energy for climbing mountains. The mountains were a far-off dream, unreachable and irrelevant. The Colorado version of paradise, then, is for people who happen to come from good families and have strong bodies. And even those who get to enjoy the mountains don't find true satisfaction in them. Heaven, it would seem, must be somewhere else.

Something is wrong with the world; it is not what it should be. We all know this. We cannot explain where we get this sense of "should," but we know that millions should not be languishing in poverty, that addiction and war and corruption and pollution should not be the realities that shape life on our planet, and yet they are. We know that the glimpses of tranquility we find briefly, in exclusive and expensive corners of the world, are the way life should be, and yet not the way it is. If we are honest, we also know something else. It is not just that something is wrong with the world—something is wrong with us. We cannot simply blame the world around us for the fact that we are not satisfied, even with experiences of great beauty. It is an internal problem. My inability to relax in Hawaii was not just Hawaii's fault; it was mine. Something is wrong with me. In fact, it is this internal problem that has caused the external problem. We are the ones who have made a mess of things. Poverty, war, corruption, pollution, and addiction are human problems; we can't just blame them on "the world." It is sinful, selfish human beings who make the world what it is. It is you and me. This, then, is the real state of things: the world should be better, but first and foremost we should be better. Planet Earth is a mess, because it is inhabited by messed-up people.

The apostle Paul is a great example of a messed-up person. In Romans chapter 7, he describes his ongoing struggle with sin. He talks about how he wants to do one thing, but does another, and how he has great intentions but doesn't follow through with them. He attributes this to the battle between what he calls his "flesh", or "sinful nature," and his "mind," or his "inner being." Inside, he has found new life in Jesus, and he counts himself dead to the sinful life he used to live. But outside, he still lives in the same body he used to, and so he finds that his victory over sin is not yet complete. He makes the whole situation sound like a miserable, frustrating way to live. It sounds like me, and everyone I know. Some people, of course, don't face this struggle at all, because they are still attracted to sin, not only in their flesh but deep down in their inner being as well. It is only those who see their sin the way God does who face this inner conflict. Paul absolutely hates his sin. By saying that he can't help sinning, he is not making excuses for it—even while acknowledging that he does it, he calls it "what I hate" (v.15) and "the evil I do not want to do (v. 19)." This is what makes the struggle so miserable, the fact that he really wants to be free of sin and all its garbage. It makes him desperate. It makes him want to cry out for help: "What a wretched man I am! Who will rescue me from this body of death?" (v.24).

We are all walking around in bodies of death. We are navigating the dangerous seas of this world in a leaky boat. We are in need of rescue, from the world and from ourselves, and that, of course, is why we call Jesus our Savior. When he died for our sins and rose on the third day, he was breaking down the doors of the prison where we were held captive, and setting us free. This is why Paul answered his own question with a joyful shout: "Who will rescue me from this body of death? Thanks be to God—through Jesus Christ our Lord!" (v.25)

Through Jesus, then, we are rescued from our sinful bodies. This is more than just the promise of "going to a better place" when you die. For a long time, when I pictured heaven, I thought only about going to a place that is better than here. I knew that Jesus told the thief on the cross he was going to "paradise" (Luke 23:43), that Paul said that "we will be with the Lord forever" (1 Thess 4:17) and that John saw "a new heaven and a new earth" when the old ones pass away (Rev. 21:1). Most of us, when we imagine eternal life, focus on external things. We rejoice that in heaven, everything that is wrong with the world will be made right. Poverty and war and all those other problems will be no more. We will be in the very presence of God, and it will be beautiful, more beautiful and enjoyable than we can imagine. In and of itself, this is incredibly good news. But it is not the whole story. An important part of the story, which we often leave out, is this: at the end of time, when God makes everything right, he will start with everything inside of us.

> I consider that our present sufferings are not worth comparing with the glory that will be revealed *in us*. The creation waits in eager expectation for the sons of God to be revealed. For the creation was subjected to frustration, not by its own choice, but by the will of the one who subjected

it, in hope that the creation itself will be liberated from its bondage to decay and brought into the glorious freedom of the children of God. We know that the whole creation has been groaning as in the pains of childbirth right up to the present time. Not only so, but we ourselves, who have the firstfruits of the Spirit, groan inwardly as we wait eagerly for our adoption as sons, the redemption of our bodies. (Romans 8:18-23, italics added).

Paul says he is looking forward to the glory that will be revealed in us. Not around us—in us. We ourselves will be glorious. You will be glorious; I will be glorious. In fact, it is only after we are made glorious that the rest of creation can reveal its own glory. There is a very real connection between us and the world we live in; according to Genesis chapter 1, we are the pinnacle of creation. We are the reason God called the world "very good" instead of just "good"; we are the last and best thing that he made, and we were given the authority to rule over every other living thing. Everything depends on us. This means that we are also the reason everything is such a mess—our sin has frustrated the whole world, and kept it from being all that it was meant to be. All of creation has been holding its breath, by God's command, ever since we brought sin into it. It waits for God to restore us, so that it can be restored, too. Someday, we will be free in a way we can't even imagine right now, and we will bring the rest of creation along with us. The laws of physics will be overruled, things will stop falling apart, and life will be very, very good again. And the best part about it, other than God himself, will not be the streets of gold, but those who walk them.

I am always encouraged when I am reminded that God has thought of everything. If you are like me, then you have faced the occasional fear that life after death will be disappointing, because God's idea of a blissful eternity is not the same as ours. But we only worry about this because our brains are small, and damaged by sin. What a relief to know that God is not only taking us to his idea of paradise, but making us the kind of people who can appreciate his tastes. How on earth can I be afraid that I won't like heaven, when I will be such a different person that I will probably be embarrassed of the things I enjoy right now? When God takes us to a better place, he will make us better people, so we can experience it as we were always meant to.

This is what Paul is talking about later on in Romans 8, when he says that "those God foreknew he also predestined to be conformed to the likeness of his Son, that he might be the firstborn among many brothers" (v. 29). Of course we will be glorious; we will be like our big brother, Jesus. John, who had an intimate friendship with Jesus before and after his resurrection, said something very similar: "Dear friends, now we are children of God, and what we will be has not yet been made known. But we know that when he appears, we shall be like him, for we shall see him as he is" (1 John 3:2). When Jesus comes back and we receive the fullness of our true identity as God's children, it will not just be a change in our last name; it will be a change in our nature. We will be like Jesus, and scripture seems to say that it is okay, even important, to look forward to our transformation.

So what is Jesus like, and what does it mean that we will resemble him? Well, first of all, it is important to say again that he is loving. The most important way we will be like Christ will be in our character, our hearts. Finally, free of the sinful, selfish garbage that clutters our souls, we will learn to love the way God loves, and we will find more joy in relationships than we ever thought possible. Every friendship, every love we have ever treasured has been just a glimpse of the sweet fellowship of heaven. And if we have not treasured friendship and love—if relationships have brought us more pain than anything else in this life, or if we have simply had other priorities—then we will finally understand why we have always longed for love, even if our lives didn't provide us with any good examples of it. We were made to love God and others, and for some of us, heaven will be the place where we finally see God's wisdom in designing us this way. The truth is that Jesus had to teach us to love, and even command us to love, because in our sinful human nature we simply aren't very good at it. As a pastor, I have observed that relationships are the one area of life that people are unable to master. We can put people on the moon and broadcast internet signals through walls, but we can't hold families or churches together. Everyone I know has been hurt by relationships in one way or another. That's why it's such good news that in heaven, our greatest weakness will become our greatest strength, and we will all find ourselves agreeing with God that the greatest thing in the universe is love.

But there is more. People were not made as purely spiritual beings; we are also physical beings. In order for God's plan of redemption to be complete, then, it must include the "redemption of our bodies" that Paul said was part of our adoption into God's family. It is not just our character that will be transformed when we enter eternity, but our bodies as well, and this external transformation is another important part of the glory that is to come. Even our outsides will be remade in the image of Jesus:

> The spiritual did not come first, but the natural, and after that the spiritual. The first man was of the dust of the earth, the second man (Jesus) from heaven. As was the earthly man, so are those who are of the earth; and as is the man from heaven, so also are those who are of heaven. And just as we have borne the likeness of the earthly man, so shall we bear the likeness of the man from heaven (1 Cor. 15:46-49).

When people meet Jesus and trust him, they change teams. We used to be "those who are of the earth," but now we are "those who are of heaven." And we are on our way to becoming like the original man from heaven. If we take this literally, which I believe we are meant to, it means that we will be impressive creatures indeed. After his resurrection, Jesus was able to appear and disappear as he wished, even showing up in a locked room (John 20:19), and yet he was physical, not a ghost, because he could be touched (John 20:27), and on more than one occasion he ate food (Luke 24:43, John 21:12). When the time came for him to go up to heaven, he simply left the ground and rose into the sky (Luke 24:51, Acts 1:9). This is similar to how he will return, flying through the clouds (1 Thess. 4:17). When John saw his old friend in a vision on the island of Patmos, Jesus was not exactly the same as he remembered—in fact John was so overwhelmed at Jesus' appearance that he fell on his face in terror.

> His head and hair were white like wool, as white as snow, and his eyes were like blazing fire. His feet were like bronze glowing in a furnace, and his voice was like the sound of rushing waters. In his right hand he held seven stars, and out of his mouth came a sharp double edged sword. His face was like the sun shining in all its brilliance. When I saw him, I fell at his feet as though dead (Rev. 1:14-17).

Jesus, in his glorified body, is amazing, to the point of inspiring fear in his close friends. While we will never be equals with Jesus, we are his little brothers and sisters, members of his family, citizens of his kingdom. God has promised to make us similarly amazing people, if we will release our grasp on this earth and reach for heaven.

Because many of us have gotten our ideas about eternity from somewhere other than the Bible, the idea of bodies in heaven may be a little hard to accept, maybe even downright unappealing. Isn't heaven too holy for something as crude as the human body? Doesn't the Bible have all sorts of bad things to say about "the flesh"? The whole thing seems pretty confusing. It was confusing for the Corinthians, too, so Paul tried to help them understand the idea of a resurrected body by using the metaphor of a seed. A seed is not that impressive to look at, and would not seem to be all that useful. But if it is allowed to "die," to be buried in the ground and undergo a mysterious process of transformation, it becomes something far better. This, he says, is what our current bodies are like: a mere glimpse of what is to come.

> So it will be with the resurrection of the dead. The body that is sown is perishable, it is raised imperishable; it is sown in dishonor, it is raised in glory; it is sown in weakness, it is raised in power; it is sown a natural body, it is raised a spiritual body. If there is a natural body, there is also a spiritual body (1 Cor. 15:42-44).

In heaven, along with renewed hearts and minds, we get new bodies, "spiritual" bodies. Some of us will receive this as better news than others, depending on whether we happen to love or hate the bodies we have now. Sometimes I think the ones who hate their bodies are better off, because they are less likely to fall in love with a shadow. We live in a culture that is obsessed with the human body; we absolutely worship it. We shape it to be as beautiful as possible and then we bow down before it. Someday we will see that we are being just as dumb as the people in the Old Testament who carved blocks of wood and stone and then made them their gods. Compared with the One we are supposed to be worshiping, the human body is pathetic beyond words. And not only that: compared with the bodies we will have someday, the ones we have now are really not worth getting all that excited about. Our current bodies, according to scripture, are perishable, dishonorable, and weak. When we set them up next to the ones we will inhabit for eternity, they are really pretty sad, like an acorn compared to a mighty oak. We would do well to remember this, to protect ourselves from the idolatry that surrounds us. Even as followers of Jesus, many of us seem to value our earthly bodies more than the eternal Kingdom of God. Apparently, we have forgotten what is coming. Paul encouraged us to think of our earthly bodies like tents: something to keep us out of the rain, but certainly not to be mistaken for home:

> Now we know that if the earthly tent we live in is destroyed, we have a building from God, an eternal house in heaven, not built by human hands. Meanwhile we groan, longing to be clothed with our heavenly dwelling, because when we are clothed, we will not be found naked. For while we are in this tent, we groan and are burdened, because we do not wish to be unclothed but to be clothed with our heavenly dwelling, so that what is mortal may be swallowed up by life. Now it is God who has made us for this very purpose and

has given us the Spirit as a deposit, guaranteeing what is to come. (2 Cor. 5:1-4).

God seems to be saying here that this life is simply an overnight camping trip with millions of other people, who need God's love just as badly as I do. I am afraid many of us are ignoring these people to stay up all night patching our tent, when in the morning we will be given the keys to a mansion.

Though we rarely talk about it, this hope in a brand new eternal body is not some irrelevant side-issue of the Christian life; it is closely tied to our identity as an alien people in this world. Listen again to how Paul encouraged the Philippians:

But our citizenship is in heaven. And we eagerly await a Savior from there, the Lord Jesus Christ, who, by the power that enables him to bring everything under his control, *will transform our lowly bodies so that they will be like his glorious body* (Php. 3:20,21, italics added).

Let me say it one more time: we don't belong here; we are different, and we are eagerly awaiting the One who will come and take us home. We belong in heaven, where we will have glorious bodies like Jesus. Right now we have bodies which, no matter what we do, will someday be the cause of snickering among our grandchildren. It is up to us which bodies to get excited about. This doesn't mean our current bodies don't matter at all; they do. When the Corinthians were getting caught up in sexual sin,

Paul reminded them that Jesus lived inside of them, and that, whatever they did with their bodies, they were dragging Jesus along with them (1 Cor. 6:15). He said "Do you not know that your body is a temple of the Holy Spirit, who is in you, whom you have received from God? You are not your own; you were bought at a price. Therefore honor God with your body" (19,20).

It is no small thing to have God inside of us. Our earthly bodies do matter. And I am certainly a fan of taking care of yourself. I like to run; in fact before I sat down to write this chapter I did half an hour on the treadmill in our host's rec room. This is partly because I enjoy being in shape, and partly because I am so high-strung that if I don't exercise three or four times a week I have trouble sleeping. We must sleep, and eat, and be good stewards of what we have been given. However, as with money, what we call stewardship can very easily become worship. We must be careful. It is not time for us to be glorious yet.

But I have to be honest that waiting for glory is hard for me. One of my favorite movies is Spider-Man 2, which I watch about every 3 months or so. Carey will tell you it is more often than that, but she exaggerates. I have always wanted to be Spider-Man. Watching him run and jump and swing from his web and lift cars over his head has never lost the appeal it had for me when I was 8 years old, reading the comic strip in the newspaper. Apparently, I am not the only one who feels this way. Hollywood has made millions in recent years by turning out an endless series of movies about superheroes. Unwittingly, the movie-makers have stumbled upon a significant spiritual truth: we ache to be more than we are. We feel that we were made for greatness, but we are limited by our lowly bodies. Any doctor will tell you that the human body as we know it is a magnificent creation, and yet it falls apart, and it falls far short of our dreams. My wife is convinced she will be able to fly in heaven. I'm hoping there will at least be skyscrapers, so that I can swing from them. Both of us, for now, will have to wait. God's perfect plan encompasses both humility and glory: humility now; glory later. Our current bodies are meant to be weak, so that God's greatness will be all the more visible.

> For God, who said 'Let light shine out of darkness,' made his light shine in our hearts to give us the light of knowledge of the glory of God in the face of Christ. But we have this treasure in jars of clay to show that this all-surpassing glory is from God and not from us (2 Cor.4:6,7).

For now, our bodies are lowly, fragile, and humble on purpose, because the world needs to be impressed with God and not us. We are earthen vessels, jars of clay designed to convey God's glory in such a way that we do not distract from it. We are unimpressive by God's express intention, and yet somehow we still manage to worship the messenger and ignore the message. God's word to us is patience. Our time for glory is fast approaching; our true home is being built.

Therefore we are always confident and know that as long as we are at home in the body we are away from the Lord. We live by faith, not by sight. We are confident, I say, and would prefer to be away from the body and at home with the Lord. So we make it our goal to please him, whether we are at home in the body or away from it. For we must all appear before the judgment seat of Christ, that each one may receive what is due him for the things done while in the body, whether good or bad (2 Cor. 5:6-10).

Chapter Five

evangelism: we come in peace

I am scared of evangelism. I am scared of it because of that feeling I get in my stomach when I begin talking to someone about Jesus, knowing that they will most likely dismiss me as a weirdo and there will be one less person in the world who thinks I'm cool. I am still going to write this chapter, because I believe evangelism is important, and very misunderstood. I also believe that I'm not supposed to care all that much if no one thinks I'm cool, because I am a stranger and an alien here anyway. But I wanted to start by saying that if you're already turned off just because of the chapter title, I know where you're coming from.

The word "evangelism" comes from two Greek words meaning "good" and "news" or "message." It is actually pretty harmless; when Christians say we want to "evangelize" people, we just mean we want to "goodnewsify" them. We want to tell them the story of the freedom and life that are offered to everyone because of what Jesus has done, and give them the opportunity to respond. That doesn't sound so bad, does it? Somehow, though, it has become a word that strikes fear into the hearts of Christians and non-Christians alike.

When it comes to evangelism, Christians break down into two groups. The first group is made up of people like me, who are scared to share our faith even though we know we are supposed to. When we hear the word "evangelism," our gut reaction is to feel guilty. The second group is made up of those who are naturally gifted by God to share the good news, and who don't understand what the big deal is, because it doesn't scare them at all. When they hear the word "evangelism," their gut reaction is to make other people feel guilty. Non-Christians also break down into two groups: The first group don't even really know what evangelism is, but pretend they do so they can sound intelligent when they make fun of Christians. The second group know exactly what it is, but would usually rather have rotten cabbage stuffed down their throats than have it done to them. Some of this is their fault, and some of it is ours. When someone's heart is hard, there's very little you can do about it. But to the extent that someone is genuinely seeking the truth about God, we should probably try to make sure that the way we deliver the good news doesn't send them running for the door.

Over the last several years, I have helped a few people begin a new life in Christ, but this does not mean that I am an evangelist. When I lead people to Christ, it is usually because they walk right into my office, and say something like "I want to know more about how to have a relationship with God." This does not happen often, but it happens more to pastors than to anyone else. In that type of situation, I am very comfortable. I am happy to share the Gospel with people who are hungry for it. And so, yes, I have helped some people meet Jesus and begin a new life in him. But I am not an evangelist. I am sort of like those major league baseball players who play 120 games a year, and along the way hit four or five home runs. They are not true home run hitters, but they do get a few, just because they get up to bat so often.

The pastor I work under, on the other hand, is a home run hitter. Whereas I lead people to Christ when they say "I want to know God," he leads people to Christ when they say "Can I interest you folks in some dessert tonight?" Right now, as I write this, he is having a conversation in the hall with the guy who cuts the grass at our church, who stopped by to take care of some paperwork. This is how my pastor began the conversation: "Have you trusted Christ as your personal Lord and Savior?" No kidding. That was ten minutes ago, and they are still talking, so it must be going well. I finally shut my door, because they are loud, and I am much more comfortable writing about evangelism than doing it. I am discovering that I like the *idea* of Christians being strangers on earth and not caring if people look at us funny, but that only goes so far. The reality is that my pride is still sometimes greater than my love. My roots in this world are still deeper than they should be. Because of this, I would be less nervous about skydiving than about asking someone if he knew Jesus when all he wanted to do was pick up his paycheck. I suspect I am not alone in this feeling. For those of us, then, who want to serve Jesus, who are starting to believe that maybe our citizenship really is in heaven, but are still nervous about "goodnewsifying" our unsuspecting friends and neighbors, I am glad to announce that there is hope. This hope is found, of all places, in the Bible, which is really the best place to go if you want to know how Christianity is supposed to work. In theory, we all know that, but in practice Christians often take their values, and even their understanding of Christianity, from culture, or common sense, or what they have seen other Christians do. The Bible is a much better resource. What the Bible actually says about evangelism may surprise you, as it surprised me when I first discovered it. I learned that the basic assumption I had made my whole life about evangelism just wasn't true. It's a myth, and it is a very freeing thing to discover that something you have always been afraid of is just a myth. This is the myth that I believed:

Before leaving earth, Jesus sent all of his followers out as evangelists to spread the good news. Therefore, evangelism is really the only worthwhile activity for a truly committed Christian.

If this were the case, as I always assumed it was, then every Christian, no matter their temperament or gifting, would have the exact same job: tell people the good news and invite them to respond. Some of us would be good at it, and some of us would be terrible, and this would provide a very simple way of determining who the good Christians are. But it is not what Jesus commanded us to do. This is what he actually said:

> It is not for you to know the times or dates [of my return and rule] the Father has set by his own authority. But you will receive power when the Holy Spirit comes on you, and you will be my witnesses in Jerusalem, and in Judea and Samaria, and to the ends of the earth (Acts 1:7,8).

> All authority in heaven and on earth has been given to me. Therefore go and make disciples of all nations, baptizing them in the name of the Father and of the Son and of the Holy Spirit, and teaching them to obey everything I have commanded you. And surely I am with you always, to the very end of the age (Matthew 28:18-20).

This is what we, as Jesus' followers in this age, have actually been commanded to do: *be his witnesses* and *make disciples*. These things are similar to evangelism, but there are some key differences. Let's look at them one at a time.

Jesus told his followers that they would *be his witnesses*. Actually, what he told them was that they would receive power when the Holy Spirit came on them, and *then* they would be his witnesses. One piece of encouragement found in both of these passages is that Christians are told they are not alone. Jesus says that he will always be with us as we struggle to make disciples, and that God's Holy Spirit will strengthen us as we seek to be witnesses. Both statements also use the word "authority," and this authority is not attributed to us, but to Jesus and his Father. God is in charge of, and responsible for, what he wants to accomplish in the world. The evangelization of the world does not, ultimately, depend upon you, but on the power, presence, and authority of God himself.

But what about our part? What does it mean to be his witnesses? "Witnessing," unfortunately, is a word that Christians have gotten hold of and made more complicated than it has to be. Don't get me wrong— I love my Christian brothers and sisters. But I am also a recovering English major, and words are very important to me. If there's anything we English majors can't stand, it's when people think they can take a word and just make it mean whatever they want it to mean. This is not as bad as when people simply make up their own words, like "orientated," but it is still pretty bad, and Christians do it as much as anybody. I grew up thinking that "witnessing" meant telling people why they are wrong and Christians are right, and why they should stop being sinners and be one of us. That is not, however, what the word "witness" means, and it is not what Jesus was talking about in the book of Acts. Being a Christian witness means the same thing as being any other kind of witness, at a wedding or a crime scene or anywhere else. It means you are willing to tell what you have seen. Before he ascended into heaven, Jesus sent his followers to go everywhere and tell people what they had seen of his life, death and resurrection.

One of the people standing there when Jesus gave this command was John. John was one of Jesus' twelve disciples, and they loved each other deeply. He must have been sad to see Jesus go, but he was also determined to carry out his Lord's instructions. He gave his life away in the cause of the Kingdom, serving as a leader and father figure for the early church. Later on, he wrote a book about Jesus' life; we know it as the gospel of John. What many of us don't know is that it is one of the only explicitly evangelistic books in the Bible. Most of the Bible was written to groups of God's people, either the chosen nation of Israel or to groups of Christians gathered together in churches. This is not to say that they have no value for evangelism, just that that was not the intent of the original biblical authors. John, however, made it clear that he wanted people to read his book and come to a saving knowledge of Jesus Christ. He explained that Jesus said and did too many things to write down in a book, but that he had selected to tell these specific stories "that you may believe that Jesus is the Christ, the Son of God, and that by believing you may have life in his name" (John 20:31). For John, the best approach to evangelism was not to argue with people or lecture people or pressure them to make a decision. He seemed to think that all he had to do was tell stories of what Jesus said and did. He acted as a witness, just as Jesus had told him to. It's pretty simple, when you think about it.

Except for us, of course, because we have not seen Jesus. What does it mean for us to be his witnesses? It means two things. First, we can still tell the stories about Jesus as we find them in the Bible, because we know that they are the very Word of God, and that they have the power to change people's lives. Second, we can tell people what we have experienced, what we have "seen" Jesus do in our lives. While we have not physically seen Him, we have, hopefully, experienced Him in a way that has left us changed people. We were not there when Jesus walked the earth, but he is here while we walk the earth.

For the disciples, encountering Jesus was a completely life-altering experience. They were never the same afterward. They could go on and on about what a difference he had made, how the Son of God had helped them understand God and themselves and the world around them. Jesus had set them free from a dead religion of rule-keeping, forgiven them of their sins at incredible cost to himself, and given them new life. He had left them completely convinced that the God of the universe loved them and was on their side, despite their weaknesses and failures. They understood that Jesus' life, death, and resurrection were, in fact, their only hope for reconciliation to God, and so they were deeply grateful that he had come. They had been rescued, delivered. They had a story to tell. And so for us, being good witnesses depends on whether or not we have a story to tell. People who haven't seen much make lousy witnesses, just as people who don't have good news make lousy evangelists.

At one point in my life, this was a pretty serious problem for me. I grew up in a branch of the Christian faith that was a little unclear on the concept of God's compassionate grace. In theory, we knew that we were right with God because of what Jesus had done on the cross. In practice, though, our standing with God seemed to depend upon us, on our moment-by-moment ability to do what was right. I felt that I was capable, at any moment, of taking a false step and finding myself outside of God's love. If any of my church leaders had ever read the book of Galatians, which speaks of the freedom Christ's followers find in him, they must have been in a tremendous hurry and skipped over most of the important parts. We spent most of our time in church talking about our own behavior, and very little time talking about God's great love. Ours was a highly stressful version of Christian freedom, a tenuous peace with God. As a result, I wasn't at all sure how God felt about me, but I had no doubt about the things he expected of me. One of those things was witnessing.

This was difficult, of course, because I didn't know what I was a witness of. I could not have put into words anything that God had done for me, because my religion was all about doing things for God. I felt guilty about not sharing my faith with others, but really it was not a faith they could have gotten excited about anyway. Good news, you can be like me and work your tail off in the hope of being good enough for God. Hallelujah. Then something happened: after many years, I cracked under the strain of the burden of perfection. Through the guidance of a wise and patient mentor, I came to see that I had never deeply trusted in God's love for me. I had a powerful urge to do something disappointing and see if He loved me anyway. I did not want to sin, but I did want to break the yoke of religion. So I dropped out of seminary (did I mention I was training to be a pastor at the time?) and became a security guard. I read the book of Galatians, and I took my time. And something happened: Jesus, without waiting for me to do something for him, did something for me, something very gracious and kind. He met me in that time, right where I was, and showed me that he loved me, not because of my strength but in the middle of my weakness. I came to see what I had missed all along: that there was no question about Jesus' feelings toward me. That had been established a long time ago, on the cross. "Of course I love you," I felt him saying, "Look what I did for you." Way back on the cross, Jesus had made the final and authoritative statement of his love for me, his favor toward me, his acceptance of me, but somehow I had missed it until now. And so, after years of being a Christian, while preparing myself for full-time ministry, I understood and embraced the gospel. What happened after that is a long story, but it is a story about Jesus, one that I enjoy telling. Not surprisingly, I found it much easier to be a witness after that.

And so this is my encouragement to you: if you feel guilty about being a poor witness for Christ, if you feel like you should do more, but feel it more as a pressure from the outside than a desire from within, it is probably best just to let it go. Give up on evangelism, for a while. Let it all go and dare to believe that if you never lead anyone to Jesus, he will still love you just as much as he does my pastor the home-run hitter, or any pastor, or anyone ever. Then devote yourself to discovering just how deep his love for you really goes. Don't sin to test him, or do anything dumb to mess up your life. Just begin asking the question, "How do you really feel about me? Will you show me?" He will, and in time, you may find that you have a story to tell, one that you are so excited to share that you really don't care whether it's cool or not.

Then something else may happen. You may find that, once you begin to discover the depth of God's love for you, you are getting more excited about heaven than you ever thought you would be. The idea of spending eternity with Him will be a lot more appealing than it was when he was just a great policeman in the sky. And the more you view life in light of eternity, the less you will care about what people think, and the more you will care about people. You may even discover that you are a genuine home-run-hitting evangelist. But don't let that scare you off.

The other thing Jesus told his followers to do is to *make disciples*: At first, this can be another confusing, intimidating term, like evangelism and witnessing. This is largely because of our failure to read the statement in its context. I used to be a pastor to college students, and I was exposed to a lot of the para-church ministry that goes on around college campuses. These ministries are led by people with great hearts, who love Jesus and are concerned about the next generation. They are soldiers and heroes on the front lines of the battle. Sometimes, though, out of a desire to make things simple and efficient (after all, you only get a few years to work with college students), they reduce the idea of "discipleship" to something a little too streamlined. Other ministries, including churches, can be guilty of this as well. Under this type of ministry, many young Christians grow up believing that discipleship means someone teaches you to place your faith in Jesus, stop sinning so much, start obeying God's commands, read the Bible regularly, memorize a bunch of verses, and then quickly find someone else you can "disciple" in this same way. There are some good things about this approach, but, as you can see, it runs the risk of becoming a little mechanical, and overlooking matters of the heart. In some cases, it becomes a lot mechanical; in my college ministry days I called it "the gospel according to Henry Ford." This is a very serious problem, because at this point we are not even offering people authentic Christianity. Christianity is not a religious program; it is a relationship with a living being, and cannot be reduced to a formula. The work of making disciples does not lend itself to the assembly line.

The disciple-making Jesus actually had in mind was something much more organic, more relational. How do we know? Because when Jesus said "make disciples" he was talking to his own disciples. From their perspective, what he was really saying was "Go and do for others what I have done for you." What he had done for them, of course, was much more than teaching them Bible verses. The Greek word which we translate "disciple" in the New Testament means "student" or "follower." At the time, all sorts of people had disciples, especially Jewish rabbis and Greek philosophers. Their disciples, who looked up to them as masters, experts in their field, followed them around to learn what they knew, but more than that to become like them. A disciple was a learner, but the word did not refer to the kind of learning that happens when we are fed information and can regurgitate it on demand, like learning state capitals or multiplication tables. It was the kind of learning that requires following another's example and then practicing, practicing, practicing, like learning to play the piano or shoot a basketball. Jesus' disciples had followed him around for three years and learned from the master teacher about life in the Kingdom of God, and now, with this new command, they were given the awesome task of taking on the role of teacher themselves, and making more followers of Jesus. To do this, they would have to take the same approach that Jesus had taken with them. They would have to call to mind not only what he had said, but how he had lived, and pass it on through their example as well as their words. This meant that they would only be good disciple-makers to the degree that they had been good disciples, good students, in the first place. As the saying goes, you can't lead others somewhere you haven't been.

I imagine, then, that when Jesus told them to go and make disciples, they probably took a moment to reflect on their own experience of following Jesus. It had been incredible. He had done so much for them. First, he singled them out and let them know they were special, loved and valued by God. Then he invited them into his life, and they began to accompany him, to watch the way he loved and interacted with people. He told them that they must repent of their sins and turn to God. He taught them how to align their values with what matters to God. He taught them how to pray. He showed them how to express God's love by meeting people's physical needs. He spent a whole lot of time teaching them about this thing called the Kingdom. He rebuked them when they were eager to judge, to put themselves first, to see people punished or excluded. He influenced them to put aside their differences and become friends with each other, although they came from such diverse backgrounds that they would surely have been natural enemies. As they spent time together, they became friends with Jesus too. They began to see that he was entrusting something to them, that he believed in them. Then he died for them, showing that they were more important to him, and to the Father, than his own life. When he arose, he made it clear that it was their turn: Go and do for others what I have done for you.

Before he left, though, he said something that I imagine must have made a deep impression on these men whose lives he had changed so dramatically. On the night he was betrayed, after they had shared their last meal together, Jesus was praying to his Father, and his disciples had the privilege of listening in. He had already said many things that night to encourage and guide them, to prepare them for his absence. Now he was praying for them, asking the Father for protection, which must have made them feel very safe. Then he said something strange:

> I am coming to you now, but I say these things while I am still in the world, so that they may have the full measure of my joy within them. I have given them your word and the world has hated them, for *they are not of the world any more than I am of the world*. My prayer is not that you take them out of the world, but that you protect them from the evil one. *They are not of the world, even as I am not of it*" (John 17:13-16, italics added).

Moments earlier, Jesus had spoken of his Father's house, and of how he was going there to prepare a place for them (John 14:1-4). Through his miracles and his teaching, he had already convinced them that he was the Son of God, sent from heaven (see Matt. 16:16). But now he was saying something new. Now he was saying that they were from heaven, too—that in fact they didn't belong on planet Earth any more than he did. Each of them could look back on an earthly childhood, and they certainly had no memory of ever being in heaven, so how could this be true? The only possible explanation was that somewhere along the way, without their knowledge, Jesus had transferred their citizenship. Once they had belonged to this world, but no more. In following Jesus, they had become like him, and now his home was their home too.

If that is what Jesus had done for them, then it is also what he was calling them to do for others when he told them to go and make disciples. Jesus commanded his followers to go out into the world and invite others to follow him, which meant, among other things, to have their citizenship transferred from earth to heaven, to become visitors in the land they had always considered their home. It meant more than that, of course, and that is the difference between evangelism and discipleship. Evangelism is a part, a small but important part, of disciple-making. Telling people the good news about Jesus and inviting them to respond is the first step. But it is only the first step. Getting someone to pray a prayer and then moving on to the next potential convert, leaving them like infants on a doorstep, is a terrible mistake. Jesus did not say "Go and make baby Christians." He said to make disciples. Early on in his ministry, he did send the disciples out with the easier task of simply delivering a message: "to preach the Kingdom of God" and "preaching the gospel" (Luke 9:2,6). But later, when he was leaving and they were ready, they were given their real assignment, which was much more relational, more difficult, and more important.

Some of you, at this point, may be feeling a little deceived. You were hoping that I was going to make evangelism easier, and now it seems I have replaced it with something ten times harder. But there really is hope here, and this is where the hope lies: Because making disciples is more complicated than evangelism, it requires different types of Christian workers. If you struggle to share the gospel with strangers, perhaps it's not because you are a bad Christian, but because you have a different role to play in the process of making disciples. The Bible actually says that Jesus made *some* people evangelists, the same way he made some people pastors (Ephesians 4:11). It is a specialized calling, and if you've got it, you'll know it. But he calls all of us to participate in making disciples. You have a job to do, but it may not be the same as mine. With that in mind, go back and re-read the above description of how Jesus "discipled" his disciples, and then ask yourself this question: Can I see myself helping with *any part* of this process God wants to take people through? Can I do any of this stuff? You don't have to do it all, because you are not Jesus; you are one part of what the Bible calls his Body, the Church, through which he continues the work of making disciples.

Many of us have been part of evangelistic efforts in our churches that place an incredible burden on the individual. We learn that it is up to us to go out and get our friends, neighbors, family, co-workers, mailman, etc., and invite them to come to church or accept Jesus as their Lord and Savior. In this approach, the primary role of the Church is simply to exist; it is the place to which individuals bring their friends when they are leading them to Christ. This ends up being pretty stressful for a lot of us. There is a better way.

Throughout scripture, there are some individuals who are clearly called to point people to God in a special way, like Moses and the prophets and Paul. But they are the exceptions. Mostly, God entrusts the task of evangelism to groups of people, specifically two groups: Israel and the church. God's plan in the Old Testament was for Israel to become a nation that made such a good name for him that all the other nations would want to know him better. They were supposed to be living evidence of how much better life is when you walk with God, and all the pagans were supposed to say, "Has anyone noticed that our gods don't seem to love us very much, and that they're mostly made out of wood? Forget them; let's go worship the living God of Israel!"

The plan didn't work, because despite its privileged status as God's chosen people, Israel seemed to have Attention Deficit Disorder on a national scale. Well, maybe that's unfair. Over time, they demonstrated the ability to focus on God for a week or more on several distinct occasions. But the surrounding nations were noticeably unimpressed. Still, God did not give up. Through Jesus, he created the church, a group of people who were bound together by their mutual faith in Him. The church was now supposed to draw people to God by its example of love and joy and peace and many other good things. The church, like Israel, was basically a group of sinners, but they were something theologians call "regenerated" sinners, meaning that they had been rescued from spiritual death and given new life in Jesus. They were filled with God's Holy Spirit, who would help them produce the good things that were supposed to impress the world. The future looked bright.

Did the plan work this time? Actually, yes. True, the early church had its home run hitter, Peter, who led 3000 people to faith in one sermon in Acts chapter 2, and at least another couple of thousand in chapter 4. God knew the church needed a jump-start. But after that, Peter faded into the background, and the primary thing that drew people to the church was the church itself. This new life they were living was so different that the world couldn't help but notice:

> They devoted themselves to the apostles' teaching and to the fellowship, to the breaking of bread and to prayer. Everyone was filled with awe, and many wonders and miraculous signs were done by the apostles. All the believers were together and had everything in common. Selling their possessions and goods, they gave to anyone as he had need. Every day they continued to meet together in the temple courts. They broke bread in their homes and ate together with glad and sincere hearts, praising God and enjoying the favor of all the people. And the Lord added to their number daily those who were being saved (Acts 2:42-47).

> All the believers used to meet together in Solomon's Colonade. No one else dared join them, even though they were highly regarded by the people. Nevertheless, more and more men

and women believed in the Lord and were added to their number (Acts 5:12-14).

I'm going to go out on a limb here and assume that I'm not the only one who's had this experience: You're sitting in church, and someone is up front trying to convince you to get out there and invite your friends to church. And if you're honest, you're thinking some version of this: "I would, if I were proud of my church." Well, maybe you are nicer than I am, and you wouldn't put it in those words. But you know the feeling I am talking about. Why are so many "evangelistic" efforts just programs that burden underequipped Christians with the task of inviting unwilling friends to unspiritual churches? Why not start by making the church better? Acts 2 gives us a model for evangelism that probably wouldn't sell many how-to books, because it is too simple, and too relational: love God and each other deeply, and people will want what you've got, and God will take charge of increasing the numbers. Acts 5 is even more radical: be so in love with God and each other that people would never consider being a spectator when you gather to worship; what is going on there is too sacred. But they will want very much to be an insider. They will discover within themselves a secret hope that perhaps they, too, are citizens of a faraway land, and just didn't know it yet.

This, of course, radically changes your role in the whole enterprise of sharing your faith, because now you are a part of a team, a team that needs home run hitters, but also solid pitching and catching and fielding, a good manager and maybe even a bat boy or two. Whatever your role, the goal is the same: together with your team, win a good name for God. Perhaps this is why we have rejected this model of evangelism, because it has more to do with the way we live than with what we tell people. Some of us are good at telling people the truth, but perhaps not as good at demonstrating the difference it makes in our lives. But demonstrating that difference has always been more important than talking about it, even for one of the great evangelists of all time, the apostle Paul.

> Now about brotherly love we do not need to write you, for you yourselves have been taught by God to love each other. And in fact, you do love all the brothers throughout Macedonia. Yet we urge you, brothers, to do so more and more. Make it your ambition to lead a quiet life, to mind your own business and to work with your hands, just as we told you, so that by your daily life you may win the respect of outsiders and so that you will not be dependent on anybody (1 Thessalonians 4:9-12).

For those of you who are unfamiliar with Paul's life, this is sort of like Billy Graham advising his fellow Christians not to seek the spotlight. A quiet life? Mind your own business? After becoming a Christian (which is a fairly dramatic story in itself), Paul either converted or enraged (mostly enraged) any fellow Jews he met by telling them that Jesus was the Messiah and they killed him, and that their precious Law was not the path to God. Next, he turned to the Gentiles. He left a promising career as a religious teacher to travel throughout the Roman Empire preaching the gospel, which was probably not the path his parents would have chosen for him. He was repeatedly run out of town by angry mobs, beaten severely, and thrown into prison. Thessalonica was one of the towns where he demonstrated his ability to anger a large number of people in an impressively short amount of time. The believers to whom he addressed this letter would certainly have known the story of how he had to sneak out of town at night because his presence had caused a citywide riot. (Apparently some people there thought he had "caused trouble all over the world"—Acts 17:6—which was only a slight exaggeration.) But his directions to those believers were surprisingly mundane: live a life that is characterized by love, peace, hard work, and integrity, so that you can win a good name for God. Apparently he didn't think that they all needed to be traveling preachers; instead, he told them to live a life that was different enough to be noticed, but normal enough that non-believers could relate to it and respect it.

I hope you find that encouraging. For me, it was a tremendous relief the day I realized that God doesn't expect me to be Paul, or Billy Graham; he expects me to be Brian, with Jesus inside. I find this easier, and at the same time harder, than my old concept of evangelism. Easier, because I don't have to be somebody I'm not. Harder, because it means that the message has to be conveyed through my life. Showing somebody how to live a new life is much more difficult than simply telling them that it is available. We have to be disciples ourselves, on the path to maturity, before we can make a disciple of anyone else. To evangelize someone, you have to know the gospel. To disciple them, you have to know God. This means that we must invest significant time in our own spiritual growth if we are going to have anything to offer anyone. No more assembly-line Christianity, as appealing as that is to busy people like us. We must walk with God, and then show others how to do it.

So maybe, if the thought of walking up to a stranger and inviting them to accept Jesus as Lord makes you feel like you just ate a bad corn dog at the county fair, you are not a bad Christian after all. Maybe you are supposed to be a stranger and an alien in a different way: in the quality of the life you live. Maybe people really are supposed to walk into your life and ask about how they can have a relationship with God, because they are envious of yours. At least, that seems to be what Peter the transformed fisherman thought. When he told his fellow Christians "Always be prepared to give an answer to everyone who asks you to give the reason for the hope that you have" (1 Pet. 3:15), he was assuming that people would notice our hope and find themselves dying to know its source. Hope, of course, refers to what we look forward to: heaven and eternal life with God. Followers of Jesus, according to Peter, are people who are excited about what lies in store for them in eternity. They are transformed by their hope, and people around them want to know more. Thus, if we want to be good evangelists, perhaps our task is not to know more or to work harder, but to be transformed. Perhaps what Christians need most, for our own sakes and the sake of the world, is to really believe in God's deep love for us, and in the home he is preparing for us. Perhaps, if we did, we would find ourselves in possession of something worth sharing, and sharing it would be the most natural thing in the world.

Chapter Six

suffering: breathing the air of a hostile world

The other night Carey and I were driving down the road in the rain. Daylight savings time has ended, so it was already dark at about 5:30. We were headed to some sort of church function, half excited to go, half wishing we could be curled up on the couch doing nothing together, which is a pretty typical feeling for us. And we were singing. We have put together our own CD, a collection of all our favorite songs about heaven, and we listen to it all the time. So we were speeding along through the gloomy night, singing along with a song by Caedmon's Call called "A New Day." The chorus goes like this:

At the end of the darkness, we'll burn these chains
And we will never be the same
We will be free
We will be free
All our tears will be swept into the sea,
And we will be free.

I was happy that night, thinking about heaven, thinking about how blessed I am to have a wife who looks forward to eternity even more than I do, thinking about how God's great love fills even wet, gloomy nights with joy and hope. I was also thinking about this book, realizing that I was getting ready to write a chapter on suffering, and wondering what I was going to say. I thought about describing some of the difficulties and inconveniences we face in our current situation, waiting for our house to be built. I thought maybe I could say something about how you can put up with anything, if you know it's temporary. That was my plan. I realized it wasn't terribly deep, but I figured the rest would come to me eventually. It was hard to think much about suffering on a night like that.

And then came last night. Last night, once again, Carey and I were driving down the road in the rain at about 5:30. This time, though, no one was singing. It was the end, or actually the middle, of a long and difficult day. For me, it started with a half day at work; on Fridays I put in three hours of saving the world before I take my weekend. In the afternoon, Carey and I went Christmas shopping. She wanted to get it done early this year because we hope to close on our house in December, and we won't have any extra money. We sat down the night before and figured out our shopping budget. This much money, minus a refrigerator (for the new house), gas and groceries for the rest of the month, divided by x number of family members, equals...twenty-six dollars per gift. Hmmm. Christmas can be awkward for us, because most of my family makes about twice as much money as I do, and they love to shower us with generous expressions of love. This is very kind of them, but it's hard to shower them back at twenty-six bucks a person. So we had spent the afternoon making the best of it, Carey discovering all these wonderful things she would love to give people, and me being the bad guy and saying No, we can't afford that. It was, as you can imagine, loads of fun for both of us. Then we had spent an hour at the pharmacy, trying to get a prescription that Carey needed, which was difficult because we are new in town and they were busy and we didn't have all the right information. Then, when we finally got what we needed, it was twice what it used to cost us in Colorado. Meanwhile, I had spent that hour slowly coming to grips with the fact that I had a nasty toothache. At first, it was something I couldn't put my finger on; I just knew I was even more irritable than usual at 5 o'clock at night when I'm hungry for dinner and I feel like a bad husband for not making more money. But soon it became clearer: I was in for a painful night.

So now we were driving down the road, in the rain, in the dark, and I looked over and saw that Carey was crying. She had turned her head so I wouldn't see, but I knew. The stress of the day, the frustration of our finances, the fact that it's been 4 months since she had a place to call home, the demands of being a pastor's wife...it was all too much at that moment. I held her hand and tried to pretend that my toothache wasn't getting worse by the minute. Two thoughts came into my head, one right after the other. First, for some reason, I thought of Paul. I had preached the previous Sunday on Philippians chapter 3, and I thought of him saying "I want to know Christ, and the power of his resurrection, and the fellowship of sharing in his sufferings" (v. 10). In my sermon, I made a big deal about how Paul cared so much about intimacy with Jesus that if Jesus suffered, he wanted to suffer, just to experience fellowship with his Lord. I remembered that place where he said "I consider that our present sufferings are not worth comparing with the glory that will be revealed in us" (Romans 8:18). I marveled at the man's perspective on suffering: it makes us like Jesus, and it's nothing compared to what awaits us in eternity. That was my first thought. My other thought, as my wife and I drove along through the night, hiding our pain from each other, was this: "Shut up, Paul."

Sometimes truth is not comforting. I have read my Bible enough to know what it says about difficult times, but in the gloom of last night, that knowledge wasn't helpful. I was fully aware, of course, that the words of scripture are inspired by God's Holy Spirit, and who it was I was really telling to shut up, but I chose not to focus on that for too long. This was easy enough, because more and more it felt like a piece of jagged, white-hot metal was lodged somewhere in my jaw, and it was becoming difficult to focus on anything else, even my wife's heartache. My tooth had been sensitive for a couple of weeks, but I was hoping it was just an old filling acting up or something, and that it would go away. I realize how illogical that is, but the truth is I didn't want to spend the money to go the dentist. For the past several years, Carey and I have been living on a budget that allows us to get by okay, as long as absolutely nothing goes wrong. If our car never breaks down, and our clothes last for decades like they did for the Israelites in the desert, we can make it without using the credit card for gas money. And now something was going wrong, again, and I was mad. I was as angry and miserable as I have been in a while, but not as angry and miserable as I was going to be later that night.

At about 4 in the morning, I gave up and went to the emergency room. I was ashamed to tell the nurse I was there for a toothache, but it had gotten so bad that I couldn't lie down, because when I did it throbbed so much it made me moan with pain and kept Carey from sleeping. I used to think the first level of hell was a Wal-Mart on the Saturday before Christmas, but now I think it is being miserably tired and not being able to lie down. The only position in which I felt relatively little pain was standing upright, but this was not a good long-term solution. And so, after several hours of trying everything else, I was at the ER. There was one other patient there, so it was only about an hour before I got to see a doctor. After filling out several forms, explaining my condition to two different people, and being shuffled from room to room for no apparent reason, I was starting to wonder if maybe I should have just stayed at home and tried to sleep standing against a wall or something. But then at about 5am the doctor came in, asked me the exact same questions as the other two people, and finally gave me a shot of something to make me feel better. As he slowly drew the long needle out of my gums, I relaxed my grip on the rail of the hospital bed, and wiped away a few tears with the back of my hand. He probably thought they were from the pain, which would have been understandable. The shot had felt like someone was digging around for the flaming piece of metal in my jaw with an ice-cold sewing needle. Apparently, whatever he had injected me with was about the consistency of molasses, because while he was pressing down I had the time to memorize the symptoms of three different liver diseases from a chart on the wall. But the pain was only part of the reason for my tears.

Like Carey, I was crying for several reasons all at once: there was the pain, but there was also how tired I was, from a long day and night of frustration and a long week of ministry and a long season of never getting to relax. There was the fact, in the back of my mind, that this day would not really be over for me until I got the bill from the ER in a few weeks, and the one from the dentist I would have to go see on Monday. There was the regret I felt from knowing that this was all my fault: I eat too much sugar, and I should have just gone to the dentist weeks ago. There was the guilt over keeping Carey up all night when she had to get up the next day and go to work, even though she would rather be home raising the children that I have not yet provided for her. My tears were tears of anger and fatigue; I was facing things in myself and in this world that I was simply no match for. I thought about Paul again, telling the Philippians he would rather be in heaven, but sticking around on earth for them. I realized what a genuine sacrifice it is, to wait around on earth so God can accomplish His purposes in us and in others. Sometimes, I thought, I just hate this place.

Everyone on earth suffers. It is unavoidable, universal, one of the realities of life on this sin-scarred planet. If you are like me, and you live in the United States of America, then you must be honest about the fact that most people on earth suffer more than you do. But you still suffer, and you will suffer more before you die. If you have ever faced cancer or AIDS or divorce or prison, or ever been abused or neglected or betrayed, then you have suffered more than I have, and you're probably a little sickened that I started a chapter on suffering with a story about a toothache. Please forgive me; I think God gives some of us less baggage so we can help others who have more to carry. But I have still suffered, and I will suffer more before I die. And I have to write a chapter on suffering, because this is a book about how Christians are supposed to be different, and suffering is one of the areas of life where our Christian different-ness is the most noticeable. Christians experience suffering and feel pain like everyone else, but because of our eternal perspective, our heavenly orientation, we need not be afraid of these things. Most people, if you have not noticed, have devoted themselves to avoiding suffering at all costs. Personal comfort, pleasure, and satisfaction are the driving forces behind much of what humans do. Suffering, therefore, which is the opposite of those things, is the great evil, to be avoided at all costs. Turn on the TV, and whether you are watching the news or commercials or a sitcom or a drama, what you will see are the fruits of this compelling desire to maximize entertainment, security, and achievement, and to minimize inconvenience and pain. Apparently, for many people this is what life is all about.

Christians, however, see things differently. When you are guaranteed an eternal paradise, and filled with God's love for people who aren't headed there, it becomes possible to orient your life toward something else entirely. There is a bigger picture. Once I heard a sermon called "Perspective is everything." The pastor asked the question "How big is your thumb?" He then told us to close one eye and place our thumb right in front of our eyes, almost touching our eyeballs. From that perspective, our thumbs seemed huge, the size of the whole room. Then we stuck them out at arms length and looked at them again. They became smaller, much smaller than our Bibles or the people next to us. He explained that this was like the problems we face: what are you holding them up next to? This is the point Paul was making in Romans 8:18 (and he was right, even though I told him to shut up): "I consider that our present sufferings are not worth comparing with the glory that will be revealed in us." What we go through now is a million times smaller than what we will experience in eternity with God. I don't believe he was saying this to make the Romans, or people like me, feel better when times were hard. Sometimes there is nothing you can do to make somebody feel better. Like many statements in the Bible, this is not necessarily meant to make us feel anything so much as it is meant to be true. In moments of pain, Bible verses may or may not put smiles on our faces. But in our clear-headed moments, when we are choosing our values and determining the course of our lives, Scripture provides us with truth. And the truth is that suffering, in light of eternity, is not necessarily something to be avoided at all costs.

One time, very early on in his ministry, Jesus was in a town called Capernaum, and he was making quite an impression on people with his ability to do miracles, namely cast out demons and heal the sick. First he cast out a demon in the middle of a sermon, then he healed Peter's mother-in-law of a fever, and then the whole town lined up where he was staying, and they had a healing and demon-expelling party late into the night. Everyone thought it was great.

Then Jesus did a crazy thing. He got up early in the morning to pray, and afterward he told his disciples they were moving on to the next town, even though he probably could have run for mayor of Capernaum and won by a landslide. The townspeople wanted him to stay and do some more healing, but he refused. He wanted to go to the other nearby towns, *to preach*! He said that preaching the good news of the kingdom of God, and not healing people, was why he had come. He actually thought that the words he spoke were more important than his miracles. So he left, presumably without fixing all of the sicknesses and demon-possessions in Capernaum (Mark 1, Luke 4). What was he thinking? Didn't he care about the sick people? The answer is yes, he did. He cared about them so much that he wanted to do more than heal their sickness; he wanted to bring them into this "Kingdom of God" he was always talking about. Rather than temporarily take away their frustrations and pain, he wanted to see them in a place where "there will be no more death, or mourning, or crying, or pain, for the old order of things has passed away" (Revelation 21:4).

Earthly suffering, then, is a reality Jesus does not intend to fully remove from our lives, because he is working on something even more important. After encouraging his disciples to put their hope in the place he was going to prepare for them (John 14:1-4), he told them plainly, "In this world you will have trouble. But take heart! I have overcome the world" (John 16:33). Somehow, this simple teaching has been lost, to a certain degree, in 21st century American Christianity. Why do we not tell children, right from the beginning, "In this world you will have trouble," instead of dreaming the American dream for them? Why do we get so angry with God when they face the trouble he guaranteed they would have? We sell books and preach sermons that promise to help people avoid trouble. We tell young adults that

God just wants them to be happy, and then we're surprised when they respond to their loneliness by rushing into marriage with the wrong person. Maybe we should have told them that people who want to follow Jesus must deny themselves and take up their cross daily (Luke 9:23), and that maybe their cross is loneliness. Maybe financial struggles can be a cross, in which case they will probably not be fixed in 3 easy steps, even if you attach Bible verses to those steps. Christians will not always succeed or be happy in this world. In this world, we will have trouble.

I know of a woman who gave up on God. Her son was a missionary in Central America, and he was kidnapped along with some of his companions. Their captors held them for years, making confusing demands and disturbing threats. For years, she prayed for his release. Then she gave up. She stopped praying, not just about her son, but about everything. She stopped worshiping, stopped reading scripture. She cut God out of her life, because he had not set her son free in what seemed to her to be a reasonable amount of time. I moved away and stopped following the story, and I have no idea what happened to her son. But I was sad for her. She could not see heaven. It was not real enough to her that she could let her son go for this life, realizing that someday all their years apart would disappear into bright, sinless, eternal fellowship. She thought God had promised her certain things about life on earth, and she was mad that those things didn't happen.

There is nothing more disappointing than having unbiblical expectations for life. This is why Paul told

Timothy to "endure hardship with us like a good soldier of Christ Jesus" (2 Tim. 2:3). Soldiers expect hardship; civilians are shocked and offended by it. The incredible proliferation of lawsuits in our society reveals that we really think something is wrong, someone is to blame, when bad things happen to us. Soldiers, however, do not get to sue someone when they get shot at or have to sleep on the ground and eat the same boring food every day. Hardship, for them, is part of the deal. Paul was telling Timothy to take hardship in stride, as something normal, rather than a violation of the natural order. Because of sin, suffering is *part* of the natural order, and we had better get used to it.

When Peter wrote to his fellow Christians, telling them that they were strangers, aliens, a chosen people and all that, they were being persecuted at the time. Those in authority were hunting them down, putting them in prison, separating them from their families, and sometimes having them killed because of their faith in Jesus. It was a scary time. Interestingly, Peter didn't tell them that they weren't praying hard enough, or give some kind of motivational speech that promised to make everything right if they had enough faith. He told them it was normal, and that they shouldn't have expected anything different:

> Dear friends, do not be surprised at the painful trial you are suffering, as though something strange were happening to you. But rejoice that you participate in the sufferings of Christ, so that you may be overjoyed when his glory is revealed.

If you are insulted because of the name of Christ, you are blessed, for the Spirit of glory and of God rests on you. If you suffer, it should not be as a murderer or thief or any other kind of criminal, or even as a meddler. However, if you suffer as a Christian, do not be ashamed, but praise God that you bear that name (1 Peter 4:12-16).

Peter, the companion of Jesus, thought that suffering was normal. Christians, who are misunderstood by this world and enemies of its Prince (John 12:31), should expect to suffer even more on this earth than those around them. We know that our Lord suffered, and we voluntarily follow in his footsteps. It is an honor to suffer with Jesus. I say this because scripture says it, more than once, and not because I always feel it to be true or even fully understand it. But Peter says that we should "rejoice that we participate in the sufferings of Christ," and Paul said that we "share in his sufferings in order that we may also share in his glory" (Romans 8:17) and that becoming like him in his death has some connection to sharing in his resurrection (Php. 3:10, Rom. 6:5). If we are predestined to be conformed to the image of God's Son (Rom. 8:29), then suffering will be an inescapable part of that process. Because He suffered, we will suffer. And the truth is that we choose this suffering, since no one is forcing us to follow Christ. Maybe this is why Jesus encouraged his followers to count the cost before they came after him (Luke 14:28-33) instead of begging them to bring their friends and neighbors along so they could go to multiple services and bring in a bigger offering. Christians choose to live for Jesus and not for self, in a world that worships self and crucified Jesus. This being the case, we would do well to re-examine our dreams of a secure and protected life on this earth. Jesus' promises to us about this life have very little in common with the American dream. Fortunately, his promises to us about our eternal life with him make the American dream look downright pathetic.

This means, among other things, that we must be very careful of how we use the word "blessed." We tend to apply this word to people who have had pleasant things happen to them, but Peter applied it to people who are so filled with the Spirit of God that the world spits in their faces. According to our culture's values, would Paul have been considered "blessed"? He once invited Timothy to "join with me in suffering for the gospel" (2 Tim. 1:8). Being familiar with Paul's life, Timothy would have known what he meant by this:

> I have worked much harder (than certain false teachers), been in prison more frequently, been flogged more severely, and been exposed to death again and again. Five times I received from the Jews the forty lashes minus one. Three times I was beaten with rods, once I was stoned, three times I was shipwrecked, I spent a night and a day in the open sea; I have constantly been on the move. I have been in danger from rivers, in danger from bandits, in danger from my own countrymen, in danger from Gentiles; in danger

in the city, in danger in the country, in danger at sea; and in danger from false brothers. I have labored and toiled and have often gone without sleep; I have known hunger and thirst and have often gone without food; I have been cold and naked. Besides everything else, I face daily the pressure of my concern for all the churches. Who is weak, and I do not feel weak? Who is led into sin, and I do not inwardly burn? (2 Cor. 11:23-29)

This is the life Paul offers to Timothy if he will follow in his footsteps. I don't know how Timothy's parents felt about this invitation; I wonder if they wished Paul would leave their son alone so he could have a nice, normal, happy life. Real Christianity is somewhat fanatical; it isn't for everybody. Christians find life on the narrow way, through the small gate, while everyone else walks the broad path to destruction (Matt. 7:13-14). True Christians are heroes: they consider it an honor that they bear the name of Christ, and live in the hope of their eternal reward. In the meantime, they walk a hard road.

I recently read through all the New Testament letters, fairly quickly, just to get an overall sense of what God wanted to say to His church. This was my impression: "Hang in there." Much of the New Testament was written to those suffering persecution. All of it is written about Jesus, who suffered and asked us to follow him. Eventually, yes, his path leads to paradise, but not before it leads to the cross. One of the "hang in there" sections that especially caught my attention is found in Hebrews chapter 11. The writer of Hebrews wants his fellow Christians to know that when they risk it all to follow Jesus, they are not doing something new, but rather following in the footsteps of the many faithful people who have trusted God in days past. When you are an alien, traveling a narrow road in a foreign land, it's nice to know that others have walked the same path before you. This writer tells about Abel, Enoch, Noah, and Abraham, who proved their faith in a God they could not see by lives of obedience, by rejecting the godless values of their world. Then he explained that they had to carry their faith to the grave: in this life, they simply never received any sort of reward that would allow them to say "It was worth it."

> All these people were still living by faith when they died. They did not receive the things promised; they only saw them and welcomed them from a distance. And they admitted that they were *aliens and strangers* on earth. People who say such things show that they are looking for a country of their own. If they had been thinking of the country they had left, they would have had opportunity to return. Instead, they were longing for a better country—a heavenly one. Therefore God is not ashamed to be called their God, for he has prepared a city for them" (Heb. 11:13-16, italics added).

As a part of my top-notch education in a fine liberal arts university, I was required to take classes on the Bible taught by professors who didn't believe the Bible was true. This was somewhat like learning astronomy from someone who thinks the moon landings were a hoax, but I did learn a lot about the way the world views the Christian faith. In those classes, I learned that some scholars don't think the Israelites of Old Testament times had any concept of an afterlife. These people teach that first-century Christians invented the idea of heaven, and that before the disciples made up the resurrection because they were so sad about losing Jesus, no one had ever heard of such a thing. For a while, I was quite disturbed by this, until I actually took time to read the Bible and discovered that it is absolute nonsense. First of all, I read about the Pharisees. Even before Jesus came on the scene, the Pharisees, who studied the scriptures more intensely than anyone, believed in the resurrection. It was only the Sadducees, who were the religious liberals of their day, who didn't. Next I read the Psalms. In their songs of worship, the Israelites' hope in eternity was evident. David said "You will fill me with joy in your presence, with eternal pleasures at your right hand" (Psalm 16:11). Asaph said "And afterward you will take me into glory" (Psalm 73:24). The writer of Psalm 119 said "I am a stranger on earth; do not hide your commands from me" (Psalm 119:19). In reading this Psalm recently I was struck with how lonely the writer sounds. Even three thousand years ago, it was hard to be someone who loves God's word; you felt misunderstood and out of place. You felt like an alien.

And then I read the above passage from Hebrews. This writer says that it has always been this way, that the hope of heaven has always been central to a life of trusting God. "People who say such things show that they are looking for a country of their own." God's people are not, and never have been, at home in this world. Everything is oriented toward our eternal destiny. Being sure of this destiny, we are set free, free to make difficult choices that may even make life in this world a little harder, because we simply have not placed our hope in this world. Take Moses, for example: "He chose to be mistreated along with the people of God rather than to enjoy the pleasures of sin for a short time. He regarded disgrace for the sake of Christ as of greater value than the treasures of Egypt, because he was looking ahead to his reward" (Heb. 11:25,26). And there were many more. The writer of Hebrews goes on to explain that some of these people found that trusting in God brought them tangible, visible victories in this life, but many more experienced no such vindication:

> Others were tortured and refused to be released, so that they might gain a better resurrection. Some faced jeers and flogging, while still others were chained and put in prison. They were stoned; they were sawed in two; they were put to death by the sword. They went about in sheepskins and goatskins, destitute, persecuted and mistreated—the world was not worthy of them. They wandered in deserts and mountains, and in caves and holes in the ground. These were all commended for their

faith, yet none of them received what had been promised (Heb. 11:35-40).

I must make a confession here. I'm sure this is an ugly mixture of godliness and selfish ego, but every time I read this passage, I think that this is what I want people to say about me when I die. I picture my funeral, and someone is up in front of the church, saying "The world was not worthy of him." I cannot imagine a better epitaph. I don't care if they mention my accomplishments, whatever they may be at that point; I don't care if they talk about what a nice guy I was, or how hard I worked, or whatever. I hope they say I was a good husband and father, assuming I get to be a father. But mostly, I want them to say that I never really belonged here, that I was like the people in Hebrews 11, who always seemed a little out of place because no matter what they were doing, what they really wanted was to be home with God. It is embarrassing to admit this, because I know it will only be a matter of hours before I do something that reveals, yet again, just how damaged I am by this sinful world, and by my sinful self. But it is still my hope.

I am writing this book in my spare time, and time is passing between the chapters, even between the paragraphs. Several days have passed now since the episode with the toothache, and yesterday I again found myself driving and singing, and sharing my heart with God. This time, the song went like this:

Just a few more weary days and then
I'll fly away
To a land where joy will never end
I'll fly away
I'll fly away, oh glory, I'll fly away
When I die, hallelujah, by and by
I'll fly away

I know that I'm not normal. I know that most people in their 30's don't look at the life that spreads out before them and call it "a few more weary days." I don't think people find me depressing to be around; I really do enjoy life. Lately, though, I enjoy it as someone enjoys a party with friends when they are waiting for their lover to arrive and take them away to a secret meeting place. I'm having a good time, but I've got one eye on the door. This doesn't mean I want to die—I look forward to a long life of fruitful labor. There are plenty of good reasons I'm still at the party. But when I dream, I dream of heaven.

In this (your salvation) you greatly rejoice, though now for a little while you may have had to suffer grief in all kinds of trials. These have come so that your faith—of greater worth than gold, which perishes even though refined by fire—may be proved genuine and may result in praise, glory and honor when Jesus Christ is revealed. (1 Peter 1:3-9).

Therefore we do not lose heart. Though outwardly we are wasting away, yet inwardly we are being renewed day by day. For our light and momentary troubles are achieving for us an eternal glory that far outweighs them all. So we fix our eyes not on what is seen, but on what is unseen. For what is seen is temporary, but what is unseen is eternal. (2 Cor. 4:16-18).

Chapter Seven

ministers: take me to your leader

I have a friend who, like me, is a pastor. He also happens to teach theology at a seminary. He told me once that if he is on a plane and feels like having a conversation with the people next to him, he tells them he is a professor. This rarely fails to bring about stimulating discussion. If, on the other hand, he feels like being left alone and getting some work done, or just taking a nap, he tells them he is a Baptist minister. That tends to shut them up in a hurry. Nothing is guaranteed to bring a conversation to a screeching halt like telling the other person that you are a pastor. It is even worse if you do this after the conversation has already gone on for a while, and the person has made the foolish mistake of assuming that you are someone just like them. In that case, they have usually already said something which, now that your true identity is revealed, they are ashamed of saying.

They will feel embarrassed, or even betrayed. They trusted you with the secret of their imperfection, their humanity, and now you have turned out not to be human at all, but a pastor.

Most people, whether they are church people or not, do not consider pastors to be real people. While many Christians may find it challenging to live as strangers and aliens in this world, pastors often find that they have no other choice. Simply because of our title, we find that we have already been labeled as aliens by those around us. We are terribly misunderstood. The reality is that we didn't start out different from everyone else—being different was a choice, and often a painful one, made out of love for Jesus. Shortly after making that choice, this is what most of us learn: serving as a pastor is a privilege and an honor and a deep source of joy, and also challenging in a way that we will probably never be able to fully communicate to anyone else.

I have not been an official pastor for very long. I have served on a church staff before, but in a different role. I was a college pastor, which is somewhat like being a youth pastor, but with more intelligent discussions, and without the hassle of parent permission slips. When you are a college pastor, everyone appreciates your work, but they don't really hold you to the same standard of holiness—and non-human behavior—as they do "real" pastors. Back when I was a college pastor, if I was playing basketball and I started to get too hot, I would take my shirt off without even thinking about it. But now I am a true pastor, which means that it might be 95 degrees out, and you might be wearing the same thick cotton polo shirt you wore to church that morning (provided you were not preaching—in that case, you'd be wearing a tie), but brother, you're a pastor, and you keep your shirt on. This has nothing to do with how strong or weak or lean or fat you are, but rather with how human you are. Any man, unless he is a model or an actor, looks unavoidably human with his shirt off. Pastors should not look human. They are like your teachers when you were in elementary school: somehow more than human, and somehow less. They belong in a certain setting, and only in that setting. Seeing your teacher at the supermarket in street clothes turns the world on its side; it just feels wrong. Similarly, seeing your pastor all sweaty and pale, realizing that his clothing hides human imperfections rather than gears and wires, can be a very disillusioning experience. In most cases, pastors are just as interested in keeping up the illusion as everyone else. So we keep our shirts on.

We do many other things, too, in an effort to maintain an aura of superhuman holiness. We learn to distance ourselves from popular culture, even the popular culture we knew before we were pastors. Right now I am borrowing a truck from the family we live with, driving it to and from the office. It doesn't have a CD player, so I listen to the radio. Yes, secular radio. Like all small town radio stations, the ones around here tend to play a lot of songs that have been around for 10 or 20 years, dating back to the time before I discovered Christian music. This means that I know the songs, often word-for-word.

So I will come through the door of the church, a spring in my step and an Aerosmith song on my lips, and run smack into the sweet lady who is the head of our missions committee, who wants me to know about the missionaries from Poland who will be in our service this Sunday. And then I feel like a sinner. Real pastors don't know the words to Aerosmith songs; our missionaries to Poland would probably be uncomfortable just seeing a picture of Aerosmith.

And it gets worse. I watch movies. Some Christians feel that movies are a bad influence because of their moral content, and they have a good point. Others of us feel that they are a window into our culture, the primary artistic medium of our time, and that they increase our ability to relate with the world around us, as well as being good entertainment. This does not mean we don't care about moral content; it just means we think it's possible to watch movies responsibly and maintain a relationship with God. There is a difference, however, between Christians who watch movies and pastors who watch movies. Regular Christians are free to have an opinion, and to defend it. If the average church member feels that it's important to watch movies, or not watch movies, they can voice their position as loudly as they want, alienate whoever they want, and there are basically no consequences for them. They may lose some friendships, but not their jobs. But the pastor's job depends upon the appearance of absolute holiness, and the pastor is everyone's friend. The pastor, if he is smart, knows that he is better off keeping his mouth shut. For this reason, I find myself not talking about movies, even movies I enjoyed, and got a lot out of, and watched years before I became a pastor. I don't want to appear too worldly, or rub anyone the wrong way.

In this way, pastors are a lot like politicians. We learn very quickly that there is a mold, a very narrow mold, which we would do well to fit as best as we can. We must be knowledgeable, trustworthy, and wise, and at the same time humble and easygoing. My current senior pastor jokes that everyone wants a pastor who is 45 years old with 30 years of experience. More than once last summer, as Carey and I were searching for our next church home, we were tempted to compare the experience to running for office. As soon as I was hired, she went online and ordered all these books with titles like "You're more than the pastor's wife," and "Living in the fishbowl." These were all books that basically started with this assumption: people are going to apply a tremendous double standard to pastors and their wives, and treat them far differently from the way they treat anyone else, and there is nothing you can do about it, so you had better learn how to cope. I suppose there is a place for that, but I am still pretty young and idealistic, so let me suggest a different approach: What if we asked ourselves "are we really being biblical in the way we understand Christianity, and church, and pastoring?" Then, when we discovered we were doing something unbiblical, we could try our hardest to make the necessary changes so that we line up with God's Word. Perhaps this is a bit too ambitious, but there were already plenty of those other books out there.

Another similarity between pastors and politicians is the issue of appearance. Like it or not, part of running for the office of pastor has to do with the way you look. When I was a college pastor, I ran around in cargo shorts and t-shirts. I was young and hip and relevant, and I felt completely comfortable being true to myself in the way I dressed. Those days, however, are long gone. The students I worked with back then wouldn't even recognize me now. I wear ironed pants and shirts with collars just about every day, except for when I wear a trust-inspiring, neutrally colored sweater. I hardly ever wear jeans. Jeans give people the impression that you haven't been reading your Bible all day, and that if they ask you the solution to all of life's problems you might not know. This is clearly unacceptable, so I don't wear jeans much. When I preach, I often wear a tie. Apparently, to some people, the tie represents a sort of a radio antenna for the Holy Spirit. It is significant that it wraps around the neck of the preacher, functioning somewhat like a collar that keeps him in check. Preaching without this safety device would be like going into the woods without a compass; who knows where you might end up? These people feel that if you are going to deliver God's word, you should do it right and wear a tie, the way Jesus and Peter and Paul did. I don't really buy into all that, but I have to admit that it does make me look like I know what I'm talking about. So I make it a point to wear a tie every once in a while, to make sure people know I am still in touch with God.

My speech has also changed. Working with college students for the last few years, I learned a lot about the English language I didn't know before, despite holding a degree in the subject. For example, I learned that just about anything you want to say can be made much more understandable to your listeners by the addition of the word "like." Instead of saying "I was at the mall," you can say "I was, like, at the mall," and now you are no longer just talking about a time you were at the mall. You are relating your story to all people, everywhere, who have ever found themselves in a setting somewhat comparable to a mall. "Like" is an incredibly useful tool, making specific speech more general, turning a scalpel into a sponge. If you are a guy and want to apologize to another guy without getting too mushy, you can say "I'm, like, sorry, man." This helps him understand that "sorry" isn't really the word you're looking for, and if there were a more masculine word for the same concept, you would use it. Guys appreciate that.

But I no longer feel free to use the word "like." Although it has many uses, "like" also signifies to the world that the speaker is not quite an adult, and probably not to be taken too seriously. A pastor cannot afford this, so I am disciplining myself to remove it from my vocabulary. A pastor's speech, like his sweaters, must inspire trust. I grew up in California, at a time when everyone used the word "dude" as both an exclamation and a pronoun. This word seems to have been permanently imprinted somewhere in the verbal section of my brain, and it still shows up in my speech every once in a while. If I'm not careful, it comes out of my mouth at the most inopportune times. If someone comes into your office and tells you about the terrible thing their spouse has done to them, and the first word out of your mouth makes you sound like you rode your skateboard to work, they may begin to suspect you don't have the solution to their problem. And so I am watching my speech, to make sure that I sound trustworthy, to keep my humanness in check.

Other changes are not my own; they are imposed upon me by others. In my new church, people call me "Pastor Brian." This is hard to get used to, because it is not the name my parents gave me. My whole life, people have simply called me Brian, and so Brian is what I answer to. But now I am Pastor Brian, which means Brian Who Knows the Bible, Brian Who Has the Answers, Brian Who is Always Close to God. At first, I tried to free myself from this label, but I met with a fair amount of resistance. It seems that people really don't want to think of me as being just like them. I get the impression this would make them feel like they were floating out on the ocean and suddenly realized they had lost sight of land. It is comforting to look at someone and feel like they can be trusted, at any given moment, to speak the very words of God to answer a question or resolve a crisis. If, on the other hand, you happen to be the person they are looking at, then more often than not you are the one who feels like you have lost sight of land, but no one knows this, and you soon discover that everyone is happier if you don't tell them.

As a pastor, I face one significant disadvantage, which is that I am young, and I look young. Biblically, of course, this should not be a problem.

Timothy was young, and Paul told him to be such a good example of following Jesus that people would have to take him seriously (1 Tim. 4:12). I wish Paul had written to the people instead, telling them to take Timothy seriously to begin with, but that is not what he did. The Bible seems to say it's up to me. Scripture rarely lets us off the hook by telling other people how they should live; it tells us to take responsibility for ourselves and let God worry about everyone else. This is a constant source of frustration to me, but I'm learning to live with it.

I am not sure that I've gotten it right, though. What Paul was saying to Timothy had mostly to do with his inside, his character: the things he talked about, the way he lived and loved and trusted God. I am working on those things, but I am facing a tremendous temptation to focus on the outside, to create the appearance of maturity rather than pursue actual maturity. Sometimes it seems like the appearance matters more, although I know it doesn't. But it's hard not to think about it. For example, I have acne. It's not terrible, but it's there. Now, everyone knows that real pastors don't have acne. When I was 13 and first began to notice it, my mom assured me that it was something that people have in their teens, and then it goes away. So far she is off the mark by well over a decade. I know I shouldn't care, but I also know that if someone comes to the church to meet with the pastor for the first time, they expect to see an adult when they walk through the door. I have had people completely forget their manners when they meet me: "*You're* the pastor?" "Is there another pastor, or are you…it?" I don't really blame them. Most people don't want to entrust the secrets of their soul to a teenager, and so we have contrived a system which enables us to forget that our pastors, all of them, used to be teenagers. If we are forced to face that fact, we might realize that we don't have anyone around who is perfect enough to meet our every need except Jesus himself, and that Jesus' plan is for each of us, in our humanness and imperfection, to help the other, as brothers and sisters—as equals. And that, I'm afraid, would make us all feel very far from shore indeed.

To make myself look a little older, I have grown some facial hair. It actually works fairly well. To be honest, I don't especially like the way it looks, but it helps me avoid at least some of those conversations where people want to compare my age to that of their children. Sometimes, I will be sitting in my office, wearing nice pants and a collared shirt, with my feet (in dress socks) up on my desk, reading the Bible, one hand playing with my facial hair, shelves of books behind me, and someone from the church will walk by. They will step in and we will exchange a few words, I will offer some insight into their situation, and they'll say "Thanks, Pastor Brian," and then leave. And I will be overcome with two emotions. One is a deep sense of responsibility, privilege, and gratitude. I cannot imagine anything more important, more fulfilling, and more beyond my ability than serving as a pastor, a shepherd of souls. I simply do not deserve this, and yet this, in God's gracious plan, is where I find myself. God help me. The other emotion is amusement. I start to imagine what I look like to them, here behind my desk, well dressed, well groomed, one finger on my temple in deep concentration as I mine the riches of God's word. They are probably tempted to think of me as a trustworthy, responsible adult. Pastor Brian. And I have to laugh. They have no idea that one part of me, and a very large part, would love nothing more than to be playing a game of Ultimate Frisbee, making a diving catch in the mud, wearing cargo shorts and a t-shirt. One regret I have about leaving college ministry to be an Associate Pastor is that I still feel like I have a few diving catches in me. Associate Pastors rarely, if ever, get to make diving catches. But I suppose there are more important things.

I have wanted to be a pastor for most of my life. I have been telling people that this was my goal since I was 17. I have tolerated years of frustrating jobs and hours of mentally exhausting classes (for which I paid or borrowed thousands of dollars) in this pursuit. I have made significant sacrifices and asked my wife to do the same. This does not make me a hero; it makes me one of thousands of people who have responded to God's call to full-time ministry with eagerness and a servant's heart. But here is my point: I have relentlessly pursued this calling upon my life for years, and now that I have been on the job for a few months, Carey and I have already asked each other at least half a dozen times "Are we really up to this?" It is overwhelming. I love Jesus and I love his church, and I know that being a pastor is a good match for the gifts and passions He has given me.

But I am not Superman. I am not seriously considering doing anything else with my life; I am just realizing that my mentor was right when he told me that people really do think pastors are superhuman. And my simple question is this: according to the Bible, is that how followers of Jesus are supposed to view their pastors?

What is a pastor's job? Is it to fit a mold, play a role, run for an office, have all the answers? Not according to the Bible. This is another area where American Christians have taken their values from culture, not scripture. As far as I can tell, this is what has happened: The Bible says that Christians, all Christians, are supposed to be dramatically different from their world. As we have seen, we are aliens and strangers on this planet. We are supposed to have different values and a different perspective on life, to make decisions differently and live our lives differently. In other places, the Bible also indicates that pastors have a unique and important role within the community of Christian believers. What we have done, somehow, is combined the two biblical teachings into one unbiblical idea. We have said, "Wouldn't it be easier to take some of the differences we are all supposed to be exhibiting, and assign them to our pastor? After all, he's the one who gets paid. He's the professional Christian." And so, more and more, we see pastors who are expected to live radically different lives, often at great cost to the health of their families, their bodies, and their finances. Meanwhile, studies indicate that the lifestyle of the average evangelical Christian does not differ greatly from the rest of society. Church leaders have become responsible for doing far more than their share to fulfill the command that God gave all of his followers: "Come out from them (the ungodly people around us) and be separate" (2 Cor. 6:17). Many Christians, it seems, believe that if their pastors' lives are different enough from the surrounding culture, then they themselves are off the hook, and can go about the business of living life however they choose.

That may sound a little harsh, and if it offends you, I'm, like, sorry. But hear me out. Pastors all over the country want you to understand something: most of the things we do, we do because we are followers of Jesus, not because we are pastors. When I read the Bible and pray, it is because I want to be closer to the living God, not because it is my job. The Bible says that no one can serve both God and money, and that the love of money is the root of all kinds of evil, and that not tithing is robbing God, and so I try not to live for money, and to give faithfully to my church. But I would do this if I were a plumber or a schoolteacher, because I love Jesus and want to obey him. When I give my time away to other people who need to know that they are important to God, even if they are not my favorite kind of people, I don't want other Christians to admire me, I want them to imitate me, because God has asked the same thing of them. I don't want them to be perfect. I just want them to be different, the same way I am different.

Pastors feel alone, and their loneliness has consequences. For a while, I felt guilty for dropping out of seminary, but I felt a little better when I learned that half of the graduates of my particular school were quitting full-time ministry within five years of getting their degree. This is not to say that there is anything inherently sinful about leaving paid ministry, or that being a paid minister makes someone more important in the kingdom of God. It is to say that if someone spends all the time and money it takes to complete seminary, they probably planned to use their degree for more than five years. Something is wrong, either with the environment they are entering upon graduation, or the preparation they received, or both.

In the past year, I have met people with personal connections to the following stories: A pastor who had an affair with someone in his small group. A pastor who embezzled money from his church. A pastor who messed around with a teenage girl in his youth group 30 years ago, and now it is destroying his career and his life. Another pastor who embezzled money from his church. A pastor who had an affair with the wife of one of the elders of his church. A pastor who committed suicide before his people could find out the dark secrets of his private life. And that's not all. On top of all this, if the statistics are accurate, there are thousands of pastors trapped in an addiction to internet pornography. The picture is bleak.

Why are we losing so many pastors? The answer is complicated, with many different factors coming into play. There is the issue of training: the Bible says that when it comes to leaders, God cares about character (see 1 Tim 3:1-13). But in America, we care about ability, not character, and so we train and hire our pastors accordingly. There is also the issue of personal responsibility, and I don't intend to let anyone off the hook for their sins. There is the issue of spiritual warfare, and the fact that leaders are singled out as targets for Satanic attack. Each of these is valid, and addressed elsewhere by wiser people than I. But here is one thing I don't hear anyone saying: maybe part of the problem is the job we are asking them to do in the first place. Maybe we share responsibility for chewing these guys up and spitting them out, because we are asking them to carry a load that no one person should ever have to bear. Maybe we are asking our pastors to get their sermons from the Bible, while we get their job descriptions from somewhere else.

In the one and only place the Bible uses the world "pastor," this is what it says:

> It was he (Jesus) who gave some to be apostles, some to be prophets, some to be evangelists, and some to be pastors and teachers, to prepare God's people for works of service, so that the Body of Christ may be built up until we all reach unity in the faith and in the knowledge of the Son of God and become mature, attaining to the whole measure of the fullness of Christ (Eph. 4: 11-13).

Or, in the NBRT (New Brian Robbins Translation): "God's people don't grow up and become like Jesus by sitting in a corner and reading their Bibles. Christian maturity happens within the context of a community, a group of Christ's followers so closely bound by their common faith that they are to be considered a single body. This unity and maturity can only be achieved in an atmosphere of selfless service, as people learn to give their lives away to others as Jesus did. But people need help. They cannot pursue this life of love and service without compassionate guidance and clear teaching. This is what pastors are for."

My job, according to scripture, is "to prepare God's people for works of service," or, in other translations, to "equip the saints for the work of the ministry." I have seen churches where pastors were doing this, where the expectation was that they would function as shepherds to those who were seeking to be like Christ. These pastors serve the people by equipping them to serve their community, either the community of believers in Jesus, or the larger community of those who have yet to meet Him. Even all by itself, this is a full-time job and then some. It means a pastor must be pursuing God with all his heart and soul, so that he can speak from experience about walking with Jesus and being like Jesus. It means he must have an intimate and ongoing knowledge of God's Word, so that he can apply truth, not just opinion, to the challenges of the Christian life. He must also have an intimate knowledge of people, and be able to help them discern what God is saying about how they can follow Jesus as unique individuals. He must be a skilled, sensitive, courageous, exemplary disciple-maker. Good, biblical pastoring, even if limited only to the requirements of this one passage, is more than enough to keep a good man reasonably busy for his entire life.

I have seen other churches, though, that must have been using a different version of this passage, which read something like this: "...and some to be pastors and teachers, to do all by themselves everything that might conceivably fall under the general category of 'works of service' until they are physically, spiritually, and financially exhausted, and their wives and children secretly hate the church with a red-hot passion." Some churches have no idea that Christians are supposed to be prepared for works of service; they think that Christians are simply supposed to be served. They have forgotten that Jesus said even he did not come to be served, but to serve. The danger here is not only that this selfishly places an unnecessary burden on the pastor, but, what is worse, people don't grow, and the world is not touched by the love of God. If we decide, consciously or subconsciously, to leave the work of Jesus to the professionals, we never become like Jesus, and our churches become incapable of significant outreach.

For a short time I worked in a church where the pastor's job was much closer to that of the priests of the Old Testament, or of traditional Roman Catholicism, than to biblical New Testament pastoring. His responsibility was to be close to God; everyone else's responsibility was to show up. We had these Wednesday night prayer meetings where we would eat a pot-luck supper and then have a Bible study. Well, Wednesday nights became difficult for my pastor because of something his kids were involved in, and it was hard for him to be there right at six o'clock when we started. Soon he was showing up at 6:05, then 6:10, then 6:15. From my perspective, this was not a problem: pastors are human, they have wives and children and scheduling conflicts like everyone else. But for the rest of the church, it was a big problem, because it meant they couldn't eat. You can't eat until you pray, and you can't pray without the pastor. I am not kidding. Every week, these dear people would stand around awkwardly, the delicious-smelling food getting colder by the minute, until finally the pastor would burst through the door and everyone would breathe a sigh of relief. He would give thanks as spiritually and efficiently as possible, and then we would eat. After several months of this, someone in the group had a brilliant idea: the youth pastor could pray! People were thrilled with this suggestion, since I was usually on time, having no children of my own and being a big fan of free food. It was determined, therefore, that I was qualified to ask the Lord's blessing on our meal. It was comical, and tragic.

I realize this is an extreme example, but I offer it as a means to help us examine our assumptions about the pastoral role. Pastors are not priests; the Bible says that we no longer need a priest to come to God. We have already seen that God views us, all of us, as members of a royal priesthood. Any need we do have for a priest is met by Jesus himself (Heb. 4:14-16), and because of Him we have direct access to the Father (Eph. 2:18). We do not pay our pastors to be close to God for us; we pay them so they can devote themselves to helping us draw near to God. We do not pay them to be Supermen, to be skilled and involved in every ministry of the church. We pay them so that they will be free to train us well, so that we can carry on the ministry of the church.

If you have no idea what I'm going on and on about, because you have never encountered this problem, praise God for your healthy church and keep up the good work. If, however, you suspect that you or your church have been guilty of abusing your brother, your shepherd, by placing unbiblical expectations on him, here are a few things you can do:

First, you can pray, and I don't just say that because this is a Christian book and you have to talk about prayer before you talk about the practical stuff. I say it because the church is a spiritual organism, the Christian life is a spiritual enterprise, and we are spiritual people. The most important things going on around us, in our lives and the lives of our churches, are the things we never see. Pastors, even when they take on only the duties that scripture gives them, carry a tremendous amount of responsibility. A great deal depends on them, and Satan is no dummy. He knows that if he can take out a leader, he can do significant damage. Sometimes I will face several days in a row when every time I turn around something unexpected and challenging is thrown in my face, and somehow I respond fairly appropriately to all of it. When it is over, and the church is still standing and I am still walking with Jesus and hardly anyone hates me, I will think, "Man, how did I get through that without making a huge mess of everything?" The answer is that people are praying for me, calling upon God's resources to make me a much better man than I really am. Charles Spurgeon, when asked the reason for his highly fruitful preaching ministry, answered "My people pray for me." Serving your pastor in this way is one of the most practical things you can do for the health of your church.

Next, you can examine the expectations that are placed on your pastor. Does he do some things that really could be done by someone else, someone who has been prepared for "works of service"? What responsibilities has he taken on that might actually be preventing your body of believers from growing up to be like Jesus? How about this one: Have you created an environment in your church where the pastor can keep his job only by being sinless, or by hiding his sin? Does he have to preach about confession, humility, and transparency, and yet fear to practice those things? What about his schedule? Does he take days off? Does he walk around with huge bags under his eyes and a caffeine IV stuck in his arm? We joke about things like that, but they make the difference between someone who is a good pastor for 5 years and someone who is a good pastor, husband, and father for the rest of his life. So do what you can. If you catch your pastor leading something like a building project or a mission trip without significant help from others, threaten him with something sharp. If your church is hiring a pastor, sit down and take a good hard look at scripture as you write the job description. Why not try, as much as possible, to be biblical about this whole thing?

Finally, you can be different. Stand up beside your pastor and be counted among those who have rejected the values of this world. Let him know he is not the only one making sacrifices for the kingdom of God, storing up treasure in heaven, living as a stranger and an alien, longing for home. We have come a long way from the church of the first century, when pastors and their fellow Christians started out relating very naturally as brothers and sisters. But brothers and sisters we are. We are in this thing together. Possibly the best thing you can do for your pastor is pursue your own relationship with Jesus as if it were the most important thing in the world. If you do, be prepared for your relationship with your pastor to change. You will lose a priest, but gain a friend, which is a very good thing, a very biblical thing. Pastors make great friends, and they need great friends. Deep down, we're really a lot like you.

Chapter Eight

death: resistance is futile

On a Friday night a couple of years ago, I was exploring the vast wasteland of late-night TV (which is a rare occurrence, I promise). One of the guests on a certain talk show was a woman I recognized from an old sitcom, which had been one of my mom's favorites. She came onto the set wearing a shiny, form-fitting dress, walked across the room waving and smiling at the audience, and sat down on one of those chairs by the host's desk, looking very slender and attractive, just the way a TV star is supposed to look. She was, of course, promoting some new show or movie she was starring in. But here's what was strange: I could have sworn that I had seen her old show, the one my mom used to like, on one of those cable networks that airs classics like "Andy Griffith" and "My Three Sons." And I could have sworn it had been in black and white. But surely this was not possible. She looked like she was in her

30's. The host also noticed her youthful appearance, and mentioned that he was aware she had celebrated an important birthday lately. She said yes, she had. He asked if she would mind telling how old she was. All across America, people like me sat slouched in their armchairs, taking our best guess. 40? 45? Surely not 50. Then she spilled it: the previous week, she had turned 60 years old.

If I had not been slouched so low in my armchair, I would have fallen over. 60 years old? I thought back to when I was a child, and my grandma was 60. She had looked, well, like a grandma. It was a good look for her, and seemed somehow much more appropriate than if she had looked like a prom queen, as this actress did. This is common, of course, among celebrities, and we tend not to think about it too deeply, because we don't really want to. Celebrities, in our minds, are a unique sub-species of the human race, somewhat like pastors, and are not subject to the same set of rules as the rest of us. We write their appearance off to good genes, healthy habits, God-given gifts, natural beauty. We are dreaming. When someone reaches 60 years old without a sag or a wrinkle to show for it, there is nothing God-given about it. That woman is about 25% post-Creator materials. She is living a lie, and we, the viewing public, are willing participants in her charade. Together, we were all pretending that people do not grow old, fall apart, and die. We are resisting an irresistible fact, lowering our shoulders and digging in our heels as the unstoppable force plows its way through our lives. We ignore death, we deny death, we make jokes about death. But death is still coming. In the end, even the finest plastic surgeons in the world cannot stop it. Everyone dies.

This is what the writer of Hebrews knew when he said that "man is destined to die once, and after that to face judgment" (Heb. 9:27). It is also what people have realized when they write sappy country songs and greeting card poems about how "life is not a dress rehearsal," and so we should "live life to the fullest," which apparently means going skydiving and eating ice cream for breakfast and asking people on dates who are way out of your league. The songs fail to mention what difference these things will make once a person is dead and either A) there is no afterlife, so they can't remember the cool things they did, B) they are in hell, where they can't enjoy the cool things they did, or C) they are in heaven, where everything is better anyway. Jesus, as you may know, also spoke of "life to the fullest" (John 10:10), but judging by the way he lived, it would seem that his idea of a full life had more to do with serving other people than anything else. Still, you have to commend the sappy songwriters for being honest about the fact that we are going to die, and that we only get one shot at life. They have at least recognized the problem, even if they have no solution.

The truth is that we all know we are going to die, and we hate it. It just seems so wrong. Something inside us senses that we were meant for better things, and yet the evidence is overwhelming: of the billions of people who have ever lived, only two or three Bible characters ever escaped death. For the rest of us, everyone who lives, dies. The writer of

Ecclesiastes called this "the burden that God has laid on men" (3:10). He said that God has "set eternity in the hearts of men," (v. 11) and yet we know that our bodies are not eternal at all. Those who live without the hope of heaven don't know what to do with this. Some people come up with impressively creative answers to life's great question in order to protect themselves and others from hopelessness, other people just have another beer. But all of us agree that death is a bad thing. Just watch any drama or action movie, and you will quickly learn that death is the worst thing that can happen to a person. Death is the thing that we hope will happen to the bad guys, while we pray that it won't happen to the good guys. If we are imagining that the good guys are real people, then of course we know that it will happen to them eventually, but we hope that this will be sometime after the movie is over, after they have had many happy years of skydiving and romantic kisses. This, by the way, is also a major flaw in most fairy tales, at least the ones that end "And they lived happily ever after." People don't live happily ever after; people get old and die, and unless they know Jesus they are eternally separated from God in hell. I told Carey once that when we have kids, I think I'll modify the fairy tales I read to them, and end each one with "And they lived happily for a long time, until they died." She gave me one of those looks that is intended to remind me that there are very few women who would put up with me, and that she deserves some new clothes and a long vacation.

I once heard a speech by a heart surgeon, who was also a follower of Jesus, who began to ask some big questions about life and death, and it led him to do something very interesting. Before performing life-saving surgery on his patients, he started asking them why they wanted to stay alive. He assumed that God was at work in leading them to death's door, and that his personal role in the universe was something more than keeping people's hearts beating so that they could watch TV for another fifteen years. The results were incredible: by and large, most people had not given any thought to why they were so desperate to live; they just knew that it was better than the alternative. His question caused many of them to re-evaluate their lives, to examine their reason for being. They became better husbands and wives and parents and grandparents; most of them met Jesus and discovered the eternal life that he offers. All because they had finally been forced to get honest about death. In this way, death serves an important function: it keeps us focused on the things that will last, namely God, souls, and relationships.

It is not a bad thing to think about death. It is not a happy thing, but it is an important thing. At one point shortly after I graduated from college, I was having a hard time finding a job. Looking for a job is a tremendous amount of work, and I was growing weary of putting myself out there only to get shot down. One afternoon I was all dressed up, with my clothes ironed and everything—something which had taken me the better part of the morning, ironing being somewhat new to me. I went to two different job interviews that day, and wasn't hired for either one. I was deeply discouraged. On the drive home, I passed a small cemetery, and was moved to stop. I got out of the car and walked around in my nice clothes, talking to God about how I was feeling and asking for his help. I began to notice the dates on the tombstones. I saw that I was already older than a few of the people had been when they died. This made me realize that I was alive because God wanted me alive. Other people had lived long lives, and I wondered about some of the things they had probably gotten worried and anxious over, things that didn't matter at all now. This made me realize that God's purpose in keeping me alive was not going to be thwarted if I was unemployed for a few weeks. Somehow, I regained my perspective as I walked among those graves; I saw that God cares about our lives and how we spend them, and can be trusted to take care of little details along the way. When I got back to my apartment, my roommate asked me how the interviews had gone, and when I told him he said: "That stinks, man; I'm sorry." I said, "It's okay; I stopped by a graveyard on the way home, and now I feel a lot better."

What allowed me to say that, of course, was my relationship with Jesus and the promise of heaven. If someone does not have the hope of heaven, tombstones are rarely a source of encouragement to them. In the famous speech that begins "To be or not to be," Shakespeare's character, Hamlet, says that the only reason people don't all just kill themselves is that they are afraid death will be worse than life. He says that no one would "grunt and sweat under a weary life" if they knew that joy and peace awaited them on the other side, but, since they don't know what comes afterward, they hang on to their boring and painful lives as long as possible. Hamlet was sort of a depressing guy, who clearly never met the apostle Paul. Paul would have told him that he was completely confident of a blissful eternity in heaven, but that he was hanging around earth so people like Hamlet could get to know Jesus and join him there. Most people you know are a lot like Hamlet. Their lives aren't perfect, but at least there is very little mystery to them. Death, on the other hand, is a mystery.

But not to Christians. Christians are supposed to be different. We know where death comes from, we know what comes afterward, and we have been told by the Living God that we don't have to be afraid of it. In a world that alternates between panic and denial when faced with death, followers of Jesus have, or should have, clear heads and calm hearts. Like suffering, death is an area in which our differentness should be readily apparent. Hebrews 2:14&15 says that Jesus shared in our humanity, and our death, in order to destroy the devil, "and free those who all their lives were held in slavery by their fear of death." We are free from the fear that keeps the world in bondage, and this truly, perhaps more than anything else, makes us the weirdest people on the planet. What could make someone more of an alien, a stranger on earth, than to stand boldly before the thing that fills the entire world with fear?

Jesus once told a story about a man who thought only about providing for his earthly future. He stored up wealth to secure his happiness in this world, but gave no thought to eternity. Then the man died, and God called him a fool (Luke 12:20). I think it is safe to say that this is God's judgment of 21st century American culture. Our technology, our entertainment, our military, and our wealth are the envy of the world. And yet we are fools, for we give no thought to death and what comes after. We are smart, but we are not wise. Followers of Jesus, however, must be wise. Jesus told this story because he wanted people to understand that life is about more than the things we own. When we live for earthly possessions and experiences, an early death shocks and offends us; it is an interruption in the life we had planned for ourselves. When we live for God and heaven, it is neither a surprise nor a tragedy. It can even be a mercy. This, at least, is what the prophet Isaiah thought:

> The righteous perish, and no one ponders it in his heart.
> Devout men are taken away, and no one understands
> That the righteous are taken away to be spared from evil.
> Those who walk uprightly enter into peace;
> They find rest as they lie in death (Isaiah 57:1,2).

When I first read this passage, I was surprised, because I had been in church my whole life and had never heart it quoted, not even at funerals. Are we afraid to say it? God isn't. Heaven will be better than earth, and anyone with any sense wants to be there as soon as God allows. This should be the reality that shapes our view of life. I have not traveled much, but my sense is that in other places, poorer places, Christians find this easier to grasp than I do here in the U.S. It is hard to dream of life after death when this life seems to hold so much promise, but when life is harder, heaven seems nearer. This is not a new struggle; even in the early church those who were "blessed" with wealth found it difficult to keep an eternal perspective. Here is what Paul told Timothy about how to pastor such people:

> Command those who are rich in this present world not to be arrogant nor to put their hope in wealth, which is so uncertain, but to put their hope in God, who richly provides us with everything for our enjoyment. Command them to do good, to be rich in good deeds, and to be generous and willing to share. In this way they will lay up for themselves a firm foundation for the coming age, so that they may take hold of the life that is truly life (1 Tim. 6:17-19).

This is what the Bible says: living for the stuff of this world is not truly life at all. The "life that is truly life" is built on selfless love, and is oriented toward "the coming age." We are commanded (Paul's word, not mine) to be unselfish with our earthly possessions, and to live for heaven. What makes this especially hard for some of us is how deceptively appealing some of the stuff of this world can be. Andrew Peterson, one of my favorite musicians, wrote a song called "Land of the Free" to a little girl in South America whom he sponsors through a Christian aid organization. In the song, "Land of the Free" does not mean the United States of America, but heaven, because that is where true freedom is found. To my mind, it is one of the great song titles of all time. But the song is even better than the title. Some of what it says I would be a little afraid to say myself, but I am glad Andrew Peterson said it:

> Because I'm just a little jealous
> Of the nothing that you have
> You're unfettered by the wealth of
> A world that we pretend is gonna last
> Well they say that God's blessed us with plenty
> But I say you're blessed with poverty
> Because you'll never stop to wonder whether
>   Earth is just a little better than
> The Land of the Free

This song has helped me because, like many American Christians, I have occasionally struggled with a secret fear that I will not get to do all the cool stuff I want to do here on earth before I have to go to heaven and be bored. But Andrew Peterson's song has helped me realize that this is not a universal struggle. When I first heard it, I realized that Christians in the slums of Rio de Janeiro have no such fears. And then I saw how silly I was to think that God could make a heaven that is better than the slums of Rio de Janeiro, but not better than the Rocky Mountains. We are safe, very safe, in living for heaven, in considering ourselves strangers here on earth. Even if I never get to go to all the cool places I would go if I were rich, even if you never have that one experience you have always dreamed of, it is all okay. We are not missing out on anything; we are just performing a little exercise in delayed gratification. We are temporarily denying ourselves in order to do something that is actually self-serving and God-honoring at the same time: investing in the eternal Kingdom of God. In this way, we are storing up our treasures for a time when we can enjoy them away from the ugly shadow of death. It is the wisest thing we could ever do.

I recently attended two funerals about a week apart from each other. They were both for older men who had died of natural causes, and yet they could not have been more different. One was a graveside memorial to a man who had chosen not to follow Jesus, to live life without being reconciled to his Creator. The service was like a scene from a bad movie; it was as if some director with no taste was trying to get me to laugh at something that was not really funny, but tragic. This was the scene: the dearly departed, who had left his first wife to marry his secretary, and then proceeded to live a long and successful life centered around hunting, drinking, and making money, was being mourned by all sorts of good-looking rich people, most of whom were there out of obligation rather than sorrow. One of these people was a tall, thin blond woman in her 40's, who must have been a niece or cousin or something like that. She was attractive, but hers was not what you would call natural beauty. First of all, she had a sort of orange-tinted tan (which was not really her fault—this is really the only kind available to people in the northwest), and her years of tanning had left her skin wrinkled and unhealthy. She wore expensive clothes and too much jewelry and carried a huge coffee drink of some sort in one hand. She spent the entire memorial service in pursuit of a little boy and a poorly behaved puppy, who were treating the gravesite like their own personal playground. It seemed never to occur to her to put one or both of them in someone's car, although she was kind enough to lower her voice to a whisper as she chased them to and fro. It is difficult enough to corral a boy or a puppy on its own, but to capture both at the same time when you are wearing a short skirt and are unwilling to set down your drink is nearly impossible. As a result, the three of them were in constant, distracting motion. Meanwhile, she had apparently put together a CD of music for the occasion, which she blasted from the speakers of her nearby SUV, and which contained mostly sappy country tunes about saying goodbye, the kind they play at small-town high school graduation ceremonies.

The pastor overseeing the ceremony was a very traditional minister, who favored the King James Version of the Bible. He read from Psalm 90 and commented about the brevity of life and about God teaching us to number our days aright, but he was very much alone in his attitude of spiritual reflection. His words about a distant God and an unreal heaven were hardly the focus, because the wind was blowing and the music was playing and the woman was walking by, bent over and whispering in an agitated tone, dragging the child by one hand and closing in on the puppy while spilling her coffee on someone else's grave. She could not have been more disrespectful if she had put on headphones and a little running outfit and done laps around the tombstone. It didn't seem to bother anyone else as much as it bothered me, though; for the most part the good-looking rich people were checking their watches and staring into space. This experience was a challenge to their very way of life, and if they weren't careful the reality of their own death would force itself to the forefront of their minds. They were not about to let that happen. All of them, from the distracting woman to the bored husbands to the hormone-driven grandchildren, had come to this conclusion: Just because one of us has died, it doesn't mean the rest of us have to face death. We just have to get through the next hour, and then we can put it behind us. What's everyone doing for lunch?

The other man who died that week was a Christian, and his memorial service was held in our church. His name was Lew, and I had the privilege, along with a hospice worker, of sharing his last hours with his wife and daughter in their living room. He had suffered greatly in the preceding months as his body succumbed to cancer. His last day was no exception, and we all cried as we watched him lie, semi-comatose, and take his final painful breaths. I read from scripture about the place Jesus has gone to prepare for us, where there is no more sin or sorrow or suffering. We sang a couple of his favorite hymns, and for a moment he seemed to respond. Then he got worse, and there was nothing to do but wait. After a time, Lew stopped breathing. We sat in silence as reality set in: he was not coming back. His family was left alone. There was weeping and hugging and more weeping. It was, as scripture says, a time to mourn.

But it was also something else. His wife expressed her relief that his suffering was ended, that he was at peace. He was, she knew, with Jesus. "He's home," she said, over and over. "He's home." There was, in the background, behind the sorrow, a very real sense of peace, even of joy. We prayed and thanked God for Lew's life, which we knew was really just beginning. This spirit continued into his memorial service the following week. His friends and family, some of whom didn't have the money or the desire to dress in fine black clothes, gathered at the church to pay their respects. Again, we read scripture and sang hymns. Then we passed around a microphone and people shared about what Lew had meant to them. They talked about how loving he had been, how much he cared about others, how he would do anything for you. They reminded each other of how he was always telling people about Jesus, how his love for his Savior was so real you could see it in his face. They said that we should feel sorrow for each other, but not for Lew, because he was now happier than he had ever been. I shared with them some things his wife had told me: that Lew was her best friend, that their love for each other had only grown in the last few months, and that he reminded her of Jesus more than anyone else she had ever known. (In case you were wondering, Lew was not a pastor—he worked in a sawmill for most of his life). In short, we celebrated Lew's life that day, and then we celebrated his eternal life. There were tears, because the man who had died was going to be missed, and we knew that his family faced a difficult road in the days to come. But ultimately, it was not a sad day. The only real grief I felt that day was for the people at the other funeral. They were the ones to be pitied.

On Lew's last day on earth, just a few minutes after he died, his wife looked at his face and told us that he didn't seem to look like himself anymore. Something had happened when his spirit departed, and to the woman who had known him for decades it was visible in his face. She said it was just a body now, not really Lew at all, and that she actually drew comfort from looking at him like that, because it was clear to her that her husband was not lying dead there in that room, but was somewhere else entirely. Over the next hour, she commented on this phenomenon several times. It seemed to make a deep impression on her; I don't think she had expected him to change that dramatically. "It really doesn't look like him," she said more than once. "I guess that just goes to show what a difference life makes." I thought about the fact that every Sunday morning I join a group of Christ's followers gathered for worship, and we remind each other that he has given us new life, eternal life. I thought that if it is true, and he has given us "the life that is truly life," then having that life in us should make a difference, and we shouldn't be afraid of death any more at all. And if that is true, then maybe we don't have to be afraid of life either.

> I declare to you, brothers, that flesh and blood cannot inherit the kingdom of God, nor does the perishable inherit the imperishable. Listen, I will tell you a mystery: we will not all sleep, but we will all be changed—in a flash, in the twinkling of an eye, at the last trumpet. For the trumpet will sound, the dead will be raised imperishable, and we will be changed. For the perishable must clothe itself with the imperishable, and the mortal with immortality. When the perishable has been clothed with the imperishable, and the mortal with immortality, then the saying that is written will come true: "Death has been swallowed up in victory."
>
> "Where, O death, is your victory?
> Where, O death, is your sting?" (1 Cor. 15:50-55)

Chapter Nine

life: searching for signs

If you have ever had to wait for a house to be built, then you know that it can be a frustrating, exhausting process. If you are told that something will take a certain amount of time, it might take that long, but it is much more likely that it will take two or three times that long, if not more. When Carey and I first got involved in this process, many people warned us about this, but we are young and naïve, and we didn't listen to them. The nice man who was building the house seemed so trustworthy and sincere. If he said something would take two weeks, why couldn't that be true?

The first thing he said would take two weeks was getting the permit. Our house is what is called a "spec house," meaning that it was not our idea to build it—the builder was already going to build it, speculating that someone would come along and want to buy it. When we came along, construction had not yet begun—there was only a vacant lot where someone had moved away the bushes to make room for a house. We knew what the house would look like, because several others just like it had already been built on the same street, and it was easy to imagine ours taking shape right next to them in the timely manner our builder described. He could not, however, start building this one until he got permission from the city. He assured us that he knew the folks down at the city planning office, and he would be able to start building in a couple of weeks. This meant, we found out, that our house would look like a vacant lot for nearly a month.

Since that time, this pattern has been repeated with every single stage of the building process. The following is a partial list of people who, over the last few months, have taken at least twice as long to do something as they said they would: our builder, the city planners, the cabinet makers, the power company, our builder again, the phone company, the road construction guys, the plumber, the city planners again, and the guys who were supposed to put up our fence several weeks ago. At one point we were told that it was very possible we might celebrate Christmas in our home, but Christmas has come and gone, and now it looks like St. Patrick's Day might be a more realistic goal. This has been hard on us, especially on Carey, who loves the holidays and wanted very much to have a home to celebrate them in. It has been equally hard on the poor family whose home we have invaded. When they invited us to stay with them, no one thought the arrangement would have to go on nearly this long, and it is putting a strain on all of us. No one talks about it, and they continue to treat us with kindness and patience, but secretly I think they kneel down every night and pray for God to supernaturally intervene and move our paperwork to the top of the pile down at City Hall.

Why don't things work out the way we want? Why is life hard? Most of us have asked ourselves this question at least once; for some of us it is in the back of our minds all the time. As Christians, we may have asked another question: Why does life seem to be even harder now that we have gotten serious about following Jesus? Didn't we join the winning team? Jesus made promises about "new life" and "abundant life." Was he just talking about heaven, or can we expect something to be different about the lives we are living right now? In the Psalms, David says "I am still confident of this: I will see the goodness of the Lord in the land of the living" (Psalm 27:13). Does that apply to us today—can we have that confidence? We know that God is shaping us to be like his Son, and that this will mean taking up our cross daily—but is that the whole story? What good things, if any, can we expect from life with Jesus right here and now?

One of my favorite Bible stories is found in Acts chapter 27. It is a great story to read if you have ever doubted that the Bible records actual historical events, because it is so true-to-life that there is no way someone made it up. It is the story of Paul's journey to Rome. He was being taken there as a prisoner, to be tried before Caesar. He and his fellow prisoners were accompanied by a number of soldiers, whose leader pressured the ship's captain to sail off across the Mediterranean Sea despite threatening winter weather. Paul warned them not to proceed, but nobody listens to prisoners. The ship was caught in a storm and driven far off course. As things went from bad to worse, the sailors were forced to pass ropes under the hull of the ship to try and hold it together, and then to throw all their cargo overboard to lighten the ship. The storm grew so violent that after three days they even threw all the ship's tackle overboard, in effect giving up control of the vessel and entrusting it to the wind and the waves. Circumstances did not improve, and "When neither sun nor stars appeared for many days, and the storm continued raging, we finally gave up all hope of being saved" (v. 20).

Sometimes hard times just go on too long, and you give up. You remember the time when you were still optimistic, and had high hopes that things would get better, but now you look back on that time and smile sadly at how naïve you were then. You are in a different, more mature place now, and you have come to terms with the fact that things may never get any better. You find that it is easier not to get your hopes up. It may seem silly, but lately there are times when Carey and I feel that way about our house. Theoretically, in our heads, we know that it will be finished someday, but in our hearts it is hard to get very excited about it. We have gotten our hopes up one too many times, told each other "two more weeks" a few times too often, only to watch the weeks drag into months with little progress made. Sometimes we just don't want to torture ourselves with hope any more.

We try not to think about our house at all, and focus instead on the realities and demands of daily life.

Some followers of Christ live their lives like that: resigned to the security of a life that is far from everything they had once dreamed, because they have learned that things are less painful this way. They tell themselves that this is how mature, realistic Christians live. They are no longer willing to risk the vulnerability of hope. It is a tragic thing to live without hope, and it would be a very tragic thing if anyone read this book and concluded that the only hope Christians have is what awaits them when they die. Great things await us while we live, but to see them we will need different eyes than the ones the world has given us.

One day as the storm raged and the ship continued to drift, Paul stood before the hungry, despairing sailors and soldiers, and promised them that not one of them was going to die. There were 276 people on board, but Paul claimed God had told him in a dream that he would safely reach Rome, and that all his shipmates would be saved along with him. He told them not to give up hope, and predicted that they would run aground on an island. Scripture does not record their response to this announcement, but if they were anything like you and me, I imagine that they were not greatly encouraged. As is often the case, God's promise did not seem to take into account the reality of what they saw around them. We know that at least some of the sailors had serious doubts, because a few nights later, as they entered shallower waters and suspected that land was nearby, a few of them tried to sneak away in a lifeboat. Paul convinced the soldiers to prevent their escape, promising that safety lay in remaining on the ship. At this point no one on board had eaten in two weeks; the incessant tossing of the ship had probably ruined their appetites, and they didn't know how long they might need to live on the supply of grain they were carrying. The atmosphere, I have to imagine, was one of desperation. Everyone was thinking some version of the same thing: we can't go on like this. Something has got to give.

Then Paul made another ridiculous announcement, this time in the wee hours of the morning, in complete darkness: their salvation was close at hand, he said—in fact no one on board would so much as lose a hair on his head. He urged them to go ahead and eat whatever they could, and then discard the rest of their provisions, reserving nothing for a later day. This time, for some reason, they were encouraged by his words and followed his instructions, acting out of a mix of desperation, hunger, and faith. They ate their fill, threw the last of their grain into the sea to make the ship as light as possible for whatever lay ahead, and waited.

Everything I read in the Bible tells me that the life of faith is not a matter of escaping from difficulties, but escaping through them. God does not prevent us from having hard times, but somehow meets us in the middle of them and asks us to trust him. Throwing sacks of grain overboard in the middle of the ocean, when you have just had your only decent meal in two weeks and you can't see any land and you no longer have any means of controlling your ship, is a fairly accurate picture of the Christian life. This life of faith is a beautiful, ridiculous, terrifying adventure with God. Once or twice I have had the chance to step out and risk something for God, the kind of risk where if God isn't real or doesn't show up, I am going to fall flat on my face. Based on those experiences, I would guess that the some of the sailors and soldiers, as they heaved the grain into the sea by torchlight, probably had smiles on their faces for the first time in weeks. I can picture them in a little assembly line, bringing the last remnants of their only food supply up from the cargo hold, grinning and shaking their heads at one another, stealing glances at Paul as the heavy sacks splashed in the darkness. "Can you believe this? This is nuts," they must have said (or at least the ancient Greek equivalent), discovering in themselves, even as they said it, more freedom than fear. Then they rested, because now there really was nothing they could do. Their fate was in God's hands.

In the morning, they spotted land, and hope returned. Paul's words were coming true. There was a sandy beach where they could safely run aground, and they still had a foresail, which is not the main sail of a ship, but a smaller one that is raised in front of the mast. It wasn't much, but it would do. They cut loose the anchors that had kept the ship from slamming into rocks in the dark, hoisted their ragged piece of cloth, and made for the shore. A favorable wind began to carry them toward land, safety, food, and rest. At this point, the story becomes so realistic that you can probably guess what happened, at least if your own life has been the least bit stormy: "But the ship struck a sandbar and ran aground. The bow stuck fast and would not move, and the stern was broken to pieces by the pounding of the surf" (v. 41).

For two weeks, these men had been on the open ocean, battered by the storm, despairing of salvation and at the same time hoping for a miracle. Finally, they were within sight of shore. They had come so close. They had begun to believe that perhaps God had not abandoned them after all. But now there was a sandbar in the way, and their ship was breaking apart, leaving an intimidating stretch of open water between them and dry land. This time, the soldiers and sailors were murmuring things like "It figures," "You've got to be kidding me," and the ancient Greek equivalents of various other things soldiers and sailors say. Meanwhile, some of the soldiers, being men of duty, came up with a quick and easy plan to make sure their prisoners didn't escape in the chaos—kill them on the spot. This would have included Paul, but God had promised that he would safely reach Rome. Their leader, perhaps now convinced that this prisoner was someone special, would not allow it:

> But the centurion wanted to spare Paul's life, and kept them from carrying out their plan. He ordered those who could swim to jump overboard first and get to land. The rest were to get there on planks or on pieces of the ship. In this way everyone reached land in safety (vv. 43, 44).

Everyone reached land in safety. I wonder, as I read that, what their attitudes were like as they sat, dripping and exhausted, on the sand. I imagine that some of them were grateful, even overjoyed, because God had rescued them, just as he had promised. I imagine that others were angry, because they had been caught in a storm, starved and beaten by the sea for two miserable weeks, lost their cargo, and then, at the end, been forced to swim those last exhausting yards to shore on their own strength. And then I have to be honest and say that I can easily imagine myself having either one of those reactions, depending on the day. Sometimes I really enjoy the grand adventure of life with God, and feel that it is a great privilege to be a part of what he is doing in this world. Other times I am just mad that things aren't going the way I want them to, so mad that I completely miss the miracle of what God is doing. Usually, when God rescues 276 people from a winter storm on the open ocean, in his great humility he uses people and planks of wood to do it, giving some of us the opportunity to ignore him, and even to complain that we had to be caught in a storm in the first place. We look around and see other people whose journeys are free of storms and sandbars, whose houses are being built right on schedule. Why us?

The truth is that my house is taking a long time to be built for one reason: God wants it that way. Our builder is not really to blame; neither are the power company or the city planners. It is what God is doing in my life. Someday, I will look back and see that this path is better than the one I would have chosen for myself. It is the same with you. If you are following Jesus, then God is working in your life to make you like Jesus, reveal his glory, build his Kingdom, and touch those around you with his love. All around you are people who are not following Jesus, who don't care at all if God does any of those things in their lives. You shouldn't compare your life to theirs, because the two things are so completely different that they really can't be compared. While you live for God's will, God's glory, God's love, and God's promises, they are living for achievement, pleasure, and retirement. On the surface, this may mean that their lives sometimes look simpler, even happier. Deeper down, though, something quite different is happening. They are dying, and you are just beginning to live. Biblically speaking, in fact, they are not even alive at all. How can you get jealous of someone's life when they're dead?

> As for you, you were dead in your transgressions and sins, in which you used to live when you followed the ways of this world and of the ruler of the kingdom of the air, the spirit who is now at work in those who are disobedient (Ephesians 2:1,2).

> He who has the Son has life; he who does not have the Son of God does not have life (1 John 5:12)

> I am the vine; you are the branches. If a man remains in me and I in him, he will bear much

fruit; apart from me you can do nothing. If anyone does not remain in me, he is like a branch that is thrown away and withers; such branches are picked up, thrown into the fire, and burned (John 15:5,6).

Paul told the Ephesians that before they trusted Jesus, they were dead. John said that people who don't have Jesus don't have life. Jesus told his followers that if they did not remain intimately connected with him, they were like a branch that falls off of a grapevine. It may still have a few green leaves on it for a while, but we shouldn't let that fool us; it will no longer bear any fruit. It is useless, except as fuel for the fire. This is a frightening statement, but Jesus wants there to be no confusion: he is our source of life, and without him, we are dead. This passage has always reminded me of the lizards my brother and I used to catch as kids. I grew up in northern California, in a small town on the eastern slopes of the Sierra Nevada Mountains, on the edge of what is called the Great Basin, the desert that covers all of Nevada as well as parts of several other states. It was lizard heaven. The trick to catching lizards, of course, is to grab them right in the middle of the belly, between their front and back legs, with your thumb and one finger. It is tempting just to snatch them up by the tail, but that is a mistake. A lizard's tail will pop right off, allowing him to run free and leaving you with nothing but a tail in your hand, which is a little spooky no matter how many times you have seen it happen. Then things get even spookier, because the tail will continue to move. It will twitch around in your hand like a frightened worm, so convincingly that if you didn't know any better you would swear it was alive. The tail is not alive, of course—its source of life was the lizard. Once disconnected from this source, it can sustain activity for a little while, but in reality it is quite dead; it just takes some time for the appearance to catch up to the reality.

God's Word says that the whole world is like that. Every day, millions of people get up and go to work, where they buy things and sell things and build things. Then they go home, where they eat meals and raise kids and balance their checkbooks. On weekends, they work in their yards and go shopping. In between, they squeeze in little bits of entertainment wherever they can find it. It is such an impressive amount of activity that if you are not careful, you might be fooled into thinking that these busy people are self-sustaining, that somehow they are their own source of life. They are not. Some of them have discovered the true source of life—they are connected to Jesus, and have received the life that is truly life. The rest are dead where they stand. All their activity is like the twitching of the lizard's tail—soon the appearance will catch up to the reality, and it will cease.

I have struggled, from time to time, with the jealousy that God's people have always felt, watching the world have its fun while we seek to deny ourselves, take up our crosses, and follow Jesus (Matt 16:24). Sometimes denying yourself is hard. We are called to say "no" to many of our sexual impulses, while the rest of the world seems to be largely unaware that this is even an option. We are called to let go of money and possessions and to invest in a Kingdom that we can't see, while our neighbors are spending their money on toys. We are disciplined while they indulge their appetites; we live for others while they think only of themselves. Often, there would appear to be no consequences for their choices, and sometimes is seems grossly unfair. This is the envy that Jeremiah felt when he asked "Why does the way of the wicked prosper? Why do all the faithless live at ease?" (Jeremiah 12:1). It is the envy that nearly caused the author of Psalm 73 to lose faith completely:

> But as for me, my feet had almost slipped
> I had nearly lost my foothold
> For I envied the arrogant when I saw the prosperity of the wicked.
> They have no struggles; their bodies are healthy and strong
> They are free from the burdens common to man,
> They are not plagued by human ills (Psalm 73:2-5).

This is the great lie, the thing that Satan would love us to believe: life with Jesus is hard, and life without him is easier. But this is the truth: life with Jesus is hard and wonderful at the same time, and without him there is no life. Eventually, the psalmist realized this; he entered the place of worship, and something happened there that made him see how short-term his thinking had been. In the long run, those people he had been jealous of were not to be envied at all:

> Surely you place them on slippery ground
> You cast them down to ruin
> How suddenly are they destroyed,
> Completely swept away by terrors!
> As a dream when one awakes,
> So when you arise, O Lord,
> You will despise them as fantasies (18-20).

Despised as fantasies. To God, the life of wickedness is not really life at all. Someday, those who lived it will not even be worth remembering. On the other hand, those who decide that "it is good to be near God" (v. 28) will continue to discover the rich benefits of the life of faith:

> Yet I am always with you;
> You hold me by my right hand.
> You guide me with your counsel,
> And afterward you will take me into glory.
> Whom have I in heaven but you?
> And earth has nothing I desire besides you
>   (23-25).

When we decide to be different, to claim citizenship in heaven by the blood of Jesus and live as aliens on earth, we receive the promise of glorious eternal life in God's presence when we die. But we also receive glorious eternal life in God's presence *until* we die. Scripture, and the many saints who have gone before, bear witness to the fact that life with God, for all of its shipwrecks, is infinitely better than life without him. This is what Jesus was talking about when he said, immediately after telling us to deny ourselves and take up our crosses, that "whoever wants to save his life will lose it, but whoever loses his life for me will find it" (Matt 16:25). All the sacrifice, all the self-denial, all the persecution and struggle that we endure as strangers on earth—every bit of it is exceedingly, abundantly, gloriously worth it. The empty pleasures of sin are not worthy to be compared with the companionship and guidance of the Living God, who has come to dwell within me. The pain of releasing my grasp on material things, changing the direction of my life, being misunderstood, being attacked by Satan and disciplined by the Father, and anything else that comes my way as a part of the Christian life, are all a small price to pay for the joy of being rightly related to my Creator, enjoying life as it was meant to be lived. I would not trade the life I find in Jesus for all the empty substitutes the world offers, which are really no more than death in disguise.

I guess this is what I have not said up to this point in the book, and it needs to be said, so that no one thinks I am just waiting around to die and go to heaven: I love the Christian life, and I find it incredibly rich and deeply satisfying, right here and now, this side of eternity. Yes, I believe heaven will be a lot better, and I look forward to the time when God decides to take me there. But I do not pray that he will take me soon, for several reasons. One is Carey.

Because this world is hard, and because she longs for heaven even more deeply than I do, I have no desire to leave her alone here. As long as God allows, I intend to be everything a husband is supposed to be, to share life with her, making the hard times easier and setting her free to discover God's purposes for her. Another reason is the conviction, deep in my soul, that I still have a job to do here. I don't want to go enjoy luxury and bliss in heaven until I have put a smile on my Master's face by making my contribution to his Kingdom here on earth. Still another reason is my growing belief that I'm not ready—that God really means what he says in scripture about making me like his Son, and that here on Earth he has a unique opportunity to do some work inside of me, work which is not yet completed.

On top of all those good reasons to stick around, though, there is the simple fact that I honestly enjoy life here on Earth quite a bit, despite its imperfections. The testimony of my heart, which I am afraid the world hardly ever gets to see, is that there is nothing else I would rather do than walk with Jesus through life. Nothing is sweeter. Nothing is richer. People who know me well might tell you that I am a little bit of a complainer, and it's true that this is one of my weaknesses. But lately I am seeing in scripture the repeated instruction that God gives his people to be thankful. We are supposed to notice the good things about the life we have been given, and be grateful for them. When I adopt this attitude, I discover how good life is. Good things are everywhere. I love spending time with my wife. I love to experience the beauty of God in his creation. I love the fellowship of the church, where I get to explore the heart of God by serving him and relating with his people. I enjoy a deepening prayer life, where I am learning what it means to share my days with my Creator and Friend. I also love playing basketball and eating ice cream; I love having neighbors; I love looking back on childhood and looking forward to adulthood. And even when I am not enjoying any of those things, even when I feel that Jesus' burden is too heavy for me and that I don't want to carry a cross anymore, I love the deep assurance that I am exactly where God wants me to be, and that in his time, and not before, I will fly away to my home. In the meantime, whatever comes my way, it is worth it.

I recently read an article in National Geographic about Buddhism. The primary difference between Christianity and Buddhism is that Buddhists believe that the source of enlightenment, peace, and happiness is to be found within each of us, and can be achieved through discipline and right thinking. Christians, on the other hand, believe that because of sin and the death that it brings, there is ultimately no hope to be found within us, that we must look to the Living God to do for us what we could never do for ourselves. Interestingly, this article happened to casually mention that increasing numbers of Christians are practicing Buddhist meditation; they seem to have no problem blending the two. Some Christians, I am sure, will respond to this with great anger; they will point their fingers at Satan and spiritual warfare, because they see Buddhism as an evil heresy. I am sure that is a part of it, but I am more inclined to see Buddhism as a poor substitute, and to point the finger, first of all, at Christians. The Bible speaks clearly about the peace, joy and freedom followers of Jesus find when they are cleansed of their sin and filled with the Holy Spirit. Along with plenty of other people, I have tasted that peace, joy and freedom, partly through the practice of Christian meditation, allowing God to speak to my heart through his Word. I tend to think that someone who was really experiencing biblical Christianity would have no interest in Buddhist meditation, because Christianity done right meets our deepest needs better than anything else. Christians who seek to meet their needs elsewhere have apparently placed some measure of faith in Jesus, but they are not finding their lives in him, as he intended. They practice a shallow, distracted form of the faith, and then become disillusioned when it doesn't produce results. They are missing out, and it is their own fault. Real Christianity is awesome.

When I was a college pastor, from time to time I would confront the issue of alcohol abuse, which is common among college students, even Christian ones. Some college ministers choose to tackle this issue head-on, preaching against the evils of drunkenness and debauchery. There is definitely a place for that. But there is also a place for saying that serious followers of Jesus don't need alcohol, because Jesus is satisfying. I was never very good at preaching against things—don't do this because it's bad—but I am happy to tell people that once you experience the richness of the Christian life, all the other approaches to life start to look pretty pathetic, and you begin to lose interest in them. You begin to know what life really is, because you are experiencing it, and when that other garbage comes along you can spot it instantly; something inside of you says "don't be fooled—that's not life." This doesn't mean you are immune to temptation, or that you don't need preachers who tell you not to do bad things. Biblical Christianity, though, is not just running from something, but running toward something. God wants us to keep our focus on what we are running toward. This is why the Bible tells us to fix our thoughts and eyes on Jesus (Heb. 3:1, 12:2). It tells us to think about things that are true, noble, right, pure, lovely, admirable, excellent and praiseworthy (Php. 4:8). Eternal life with Jesus is full of those kinds of things, and when your life starts to fill up with things like that, you wouldn't trade them for a drunken party in a million years.

If you are like me, when someone talks about "eternal" or "everlasting" life, your mind immediately jumps to thoughts of life after death. We are used to using these words at funerals, or perhaps at times when we are sharing our faith with others, if we are courageous enough to do such a thing. Only recently have I realized that when I think about eternal life, too often I completely skip over the life that I am living right now. It is a new thought for me that nothing in these words refers specifically to heaven, but instead to the uninterrupted life-to-the-fullest which begins right now, as soon as we entrust ourselves to Jesus our Savior. My pastor likes to say that if this weren't true, Jesus would have promised us "intermittent life"—life right now on earth until we die, and then later on in heaven more life, of a different sort. This, however, is not what we are promised. They are one and the same, this life we enjoy on earth and the life we will enjoy in heaven. Eternal life begins now. The absence of sin and death will obviously make some things a lot different when we get to heaven. But it will be the same life. We will enjoy new bodies, and a new heaven and a new earth, and the very presence of God, and many other wonderful things. But they will not be completely unfamiliar things. We can taste them now. If we are not tasting them now, then we have not really discovered the life Jesus came to offer.

Jesus had a lot to say about his offer of life, and the following passages are a sample. As you meditate on them, let me suggest that you pray the following prayer, or something like it: "Jesus, I confess that I have sinned by seeking life everywhere but in you. Please forgive me, and teach me to receive and enjoy the life you died to give me, from this day on."

> Everyone who drinks this (earthly) water will be thirsty again, but whoever drinks the water I give him will never thirst. Indeed, the water I give him will become in him a spring of water welling up to eternal life (John 4:13,14).

> I tell you the truth, whoever hears my word and believes him who sent me has eternal life and

will not be condemned; he has crossed over from death to life (John 5:24).

I am the bread of life. He who comes to me will never go hungry, and he who believes in me will never be thirsty (John 6:35).

Whoever eats my flesh and drinks my blood has eternal life, and I will raise him up at the last day (John 6:54).

The thief comes only to steal and kill and destroy. I have come that they may have life, and have it to the full (John 10:10).

My sheep listen to my voice; I know them, and they follow me. I give them eternal life, and they shall never perish; no one can snatch them out of my hand (John 10:28).

I am the resurrection and the life. He who believes in me will live, even though he dies; and whoever lives and believes in me will never die. Do you believe this? (John 11:25,26).

Father, the time has come. Glorify your son, that your Son may glorify you. For you granted him authority over all people that he might give eternal life to all those you have given him. Now this is eternal life: that they may know you, the only true God, and Jesus Christ, whom you have sent (John 17:1-3).

Chapter Ten

heaven: the house on Neptune

I caught my dad being sentimental the other day. This might not sound like a big deal, unless you know my dad, who happens to be the toughest person alive. My entire life, I have lived in awe of this man who has always seemed like so much more of a man than I could ever be. He is not only strong, but completely self-reliant. Growing up, I honestly didn't know that some people in the world have to hire others to help them fix things, because we never had to do that. My dad can replace an engine, build a deck, install a gas furnace, or re-wire an entire house with about as much effort as it takes me to mow the lawn or hang a picture on the wall. He is a genius with his hands. When I was young, he worked in sawmills or in the woods for logging companies. Then he decided it was time to settle down, so he became a correctional officer at a big state prison in California. It was common, when I was in junior high, for my dad to come home with big bruises on his shoulders from training with his side-handle baton, or to not come home at all because he had been called upon to work a "double," which meant one eight-hour shift right after another. When we asked him if he was tired, he'd say "nah." When we asked him if the bruises hurt, he would just smile and say "You should see the other guy." I would smile too, secure in the knowledge that my dad was a real-life Bruce Willis, and return to my homework.

Early on, it became clear that I was not going to be my dad; I was going to turn out to be one of those guys who has to hire people to fix things. While my brother Randy was in the garage with Dad, learning how to replace an alternator or something, I was inside at my desk, studying. When it comes to car repair, I am intimidated by the thought of changing my own oil. On the other hand, I write better poetry than either Dad or Randy. My dad never made me feel badly about my lack of mechanical ability; he always encouraged me to follow my heart and be myself. Still, I always felt like something was wrong with me, because I have been known to shed a tear or two at the end of a touching movie, whereas the only time my dad cries is when they have to use tear gas to put down a riot at the prison. After nearly 20 years on the job, my dad, who is now a lieutenant, no longer wears a gas mask for these incidents; he considers a mask to be a nuisance. Like I said, my dad is tough.

A few years ago Dad slid his Harley Davidson under a barbed-wire fence at about 60 miles an hour.

It didn't quite fit. Fortunately, he was wearing a jacket and a helmet, which saved his life. But the visor on his helmet was not pulled down over his face. After walking half a mile to the nearest farmhouse, holding his face on with a rag, he gave the people there, who were having a barbeque at the time, clear instructions about what to tell the paramedics, and then he passed out on their lawn. Later, they were able to find his bike by following the trail of blood back to the scene of the accident. He ended up losing about half the blood in his body, and underwent seven hours of reconstructive surgery as doctors worked to put him back together, followed by several more surgeries in the weeks that followed. Randy and I went to see him in the hospital, but I will spare you the description of his cuts and bruises, and the various tubes that were inserted into him, different tubes for different reasons. He was a mess. Still, he smiled when we entered. "You should see the other guy," he said. He told us the story of the accident and answered our questions about his injuries, assuring us that it wasn't as bad as it looked. Throughout the whole ordeal, he never cried. But I did.

More recently, Dad was undergoing a medical treatment that required him to give himself shots every couple of days. These shots made him absolutely miserable, and caused him to be less than his normal cheerful self. The longer his treatment went on, the shorter his temper became. As a lieutenant, he was responsible for holding hearings and determining the severity of the punishments given to inmates who broke various rules. He developed a reputation as the lieutenant you hoped you didn't get, and according to rumors, inmates who were unlucky enough to be called before Lieutenant Robbins could be seen crossing themselves and looking skyward before entering his office, and not just the Catholics, either. In this way, although he is not a follower of Jesus, my dad was responsible for helping many Christians discover new levels of sincerity in the practice of their faith. Having been called into his office once or twice myself in my younger years, I can't blame them.

Perhaps now you can see why it was a big deal to catch my dad being sentimental. It is far from a common occurrence. This was the situation: Mom and Dad were visiting me and Carey here on the coast, and one day we went down to a nearby harbor to shop and eat and be tourists. Toward the end of the day, when we could shop and eat no more, we found ourselves near the entrance to the docks where the big fishing boats are. It was raining lightly, and Mom and Carey were tired, so they decided to wait in the car while Dad and I went for a little walk to look at the boats. Dad had been a commercial fisherman before I was born, but I knew very little about those years. Walking among the boats, he began to point out things I would never have noticed, like how different ships were rigged for different types of fish. He seemed to know everything, and I was impressed—I had not known that fishing had been such a significant part of his life. The more he talked about it, the more something inside of him seemed to be awakening from a long slumber, so I pressed him for more

The House on Neptune

details about this other life he had lived. Soon he was telling stories of storms and sharks and dolphins, of days and nights and months at sea. He spoke of the incredible sense of freedom he always had when setting out from the harbor. In those moments, with the land shrinking behind him, he was escaping rules and restrictions, leaving behind the world of school, church and authority that he disliked so much. Real life, life worth living, was found on the open ocean, where no one could tell you what to do, and all that mattered was working hard with your own two hands. Even in the storms, when the boat became a tiny speck tossed among the mighty waves, he felt alive and free in a way he had never felt since. I began to see that, in some ways, those years of fishing were the happiest of Dad's life.

At one point, we passed some young guys who were getting ready to set out the next morning, loading supplies from a truck onto their boat. Dad nodded in their direction, and said to me, "I've done that a few times." And that was it, the sentimental moment. If you didn't know him, you might have missed it, but to me it was clear. He might as well have said "I wish I was going with them." He started up a brief conversation with them about how far out they were going, which fish were biting this time of year, and things like that. They were strong young men, who laughed and joked as they hoisted heavy loads over the side of their boat. He watched them over his shoulder as we walked away, and then confessed to me that he thought maybe his life of wrestling logs in the woods and inmates in the prison had been an ongoing attempt to recapture the perfect blend of hard work and adventure he had experienced as a fisherman. "There's just nothing else like it," he said. For a moment, we both stood and pictured Dad as a younger man, working long days with hooks and nets in the cold water until his hands ached and his legs trembled, testing his strength and wits against the ocean. We saw him heading out of the harbor at the start of another trip, miles of endless water on the horizon, spray coming over the sides of the boat. We saw him exchanging tedium and security for a life of adventure on the high seas, the life he felt he was made to live, the life that he wanted to live forever. We both knew, of course, that it was the life he had given up when I was born.

And here is the real tragedy: my dad has been around Christians his whole life, but he has never heard anything about heaven that has made him think he might want to go there. Given the choice, he would rather go fishing. He has heard many sermons, some of them far too long, about Jesus and the new life that he offers. But the Christians he knows have left him unconvinced that this life is as good as the Bible says it is. On the other hand, after talking to him for ten minutes I was seriously tempted to drop everything and become a fisherman. Without trying, in a matter of moments, he sold me on an entire lifestyle, simply by relating his own experience with honesty, from his heart. This happens to me from time to time. Usually I am quite confident of my calling as a minister of God's Word, but a few months ago I saw a movie that had me seriously considering being a fireman for the better part of an afternoon. It did not do this by presenting me with a page full of facts about being a fireman, but by showing me what it is like; it painted a picture, and I came away with the overwhelming feeling that *I want to experience that*. I know that my dad is a sinner who has turned from God like the rest of us, and that he is ultimately responsible for his own choice about what to do with Jesus. But for my part, I pray that someday he might encounter a picture of the Christian life that rivals his best days on the ocean, that invites him to embrace something not only true, but genuinely desirable.

Fishing, after all, is not heaven. If you press my dad further, you will soon discover a dark side to all the romantic stories. You will hear about the broken families, miserable finances, and failing health that plague most of the men who answer the call of the sea. Fishermen's wives, for example, might tell you that a little tedium and security might not be such a bad thing when it comes to paying bills and raising children. There is also the reality of competition from bigger boats, increasing government regulations, the rising cost of fuel and the falling price of fish. My dad might tell you about the guys he knew who lost their lives, or about the permanent damage to his wrists he earned while wrestling all that heavy equipment. It is no paradise. Fishing, like everything else in this world, is tainted by sin and conducted under the ever-present shadow of death. Heaven will be better.

Earlier today I was playing flag football with a bunch of guys I don't know very well yet. I didn't introduce myself as a pastor, and I certainly didn't distinguish myself as any sort of football star. When I left, those guys probably thought of me as a normal person, like them, if they thought of me at all. Several of them were definitely not followers of Jesus, and I prayed that by my conduct I might be some sort of a light that would point them to Christ, but I honestly don't know if anyone noticed. As I drove home, I started wondering if anything will ever come of this book, and if they might read it someday, and realize that it was me who wrote it, and if they would be disappointed that I had been so deceptively normal. I am not trying to hide my Christian faith, I just don't always know how to show it very well. It is easy to say all of these things about being a citizen of heaven, a stranger and an alien on earth, because it is all in the Bible, and I know that it is true. But I still get discouraged about how we're ever going to make our house payments, and I still get mad at myself when I let somebody get past me and he scores a touchdown. Like most Christians, I am still trying to figure out exactly how I am supposed to view the world in which I find myself. The Bible, after all, says two different things about the world, which can seem to be pretty contradictory. On the one hand, it seems to say that the world is bad, and Jesus' followers don't belong here:

> Do not love the world or anything in the world. If anyone loves the world, the love of the Father is not in him. For everything in the world—the cravings of sinful man, the lust of his eyes and

the boasting of what he has and does—comes not from the Father but from the world. The world and its desires pass away, but the man who does the will of God lives forever (1 John 2:15-17).

You do not belong to the world, but I have chosen you out of the world. That is why the world hates you (John 15:19).

On the other hand, there is at least one place where scripture seems to say that the world is incredibly precious; it is so valuable to God, in fact, that he was willing to sacrifice his only Son for it: "For God so loved the world that he gave his one and only Son, that whoever believes in him shall not perish but have eternal life" (John 3:16). So is God for this world, or against it? How are his people supposed to feel about it? Interestingly enough, these passages of scripture were all recorded by the same human author. John was clearly aware that God loved the world enough to send his Son to die for it, and yet he also felt that there is something about the world that followers of Jesus are not supposed to love at all.

In my clearer moments, of course, I understand that what God loves about the world is people, and what He hates about it is sin and death and everything they have done to his beloved creation. But in other moments, I get it backwards, and I do not love people all that much, and I am far too attracted to a lot of silly garbage. Slowly, I am getting better. One thing that helps me get better is the realization that, over and over again, the Bible gives the same reason for releasing my grasp on the things of this world: they will not last. Out of all the bad things John could say about the desires of this world, he chooses to focus on the fact that they pass away; they come to an end. But, he points out, the man who does the will of God does not come to an end; he lives forever. In the same way, Jesus told Nicodemus that God sent his one and only Son so that those who believe in him will not die, but live forever. In both cases, eternity is the point. God wants us to get excited about eternity. Seen this way, I suppose, these statements are not that contradictory after all. Perhaps, then, this is how Jesus' followers are supposed to view the world: we are to view it from the perspective of forever. Forever makes us love the world, because God made it, and because it is full of precious people with eternal souls. Forever also keeps us from loving the world, because it will not last much longer. I know that this is hard, that some days it all seems like too much, and you feel like you don't want to love the world or hate the world, you just want to go fishing. On days like that, you should probably go fishing. But part of you should be dreaming of heaven as you go.

When I was in college, I led a small Bible study for a group of guys in my dorm. We came from diverse backgrounds: some Catholic, some Protestant, some agnostic. We became much more diverse, however, when an older guy named Vinnie joined our group. Vinnie was Catholic, but he was much more than that. Vinnie was what is called a Novice, or a priest in training. He looked like us, and talked like us, and seemed like a perfectly normal guy in every way, except for the small fact that he was charging ahead with a plan to voluntarily give up sex for the love of God. Because of this, we admired Vinnie, but at the same time we thought he was sort of a freak. The life of sacrifice he was entering into was more than a group of 20-year-olds could fathom. Still, the guys enjoyed having him in the group, and so did I, although I was a little intimidated to lead a study in which one of the members had been receiving theological training for the past 7 years. Vinnie was gracious and humble, though, and let me lead, occasionally contributing some insight about life with God that was the one thing we would all leave thinking about that night. After several months, the big day came, and we were all invited to attend. Vinnie wanted us there when he made his vows and became a priest.

I must confess that when the guys and I pictured this event in our minds, we imagined something like a funeral. As far as we were concerned, it was the end of poor Vinnie's life. To our surprise, we found that the ceremony was more like a wedding than anything else. Vinnie marched down the aisle all by himself in elegant robes, and knelt in front of the minister, who led him through his vows: poverty, chastity, and obedience. I thought about weddings I had been to, and the vows I had heard there: for richer or for poorer, for better or for worse, in sickness and in health, forsaking all others. It was like Vinnie was getting married, except that no one else was standing there, only Jesus. It was beautiful. The best part, though, was at the end. The minister explained that, at Vinnie's request, we were all to stand and sing as he marched back down the aisle and out the door; we were performing the recessional. At that point, the atmosphere in the room became decidedly un-Catholic. What had been a solemn ceremony became a party. Vinnie had united himself to his Lord, and we were celebrating with them. We sang and clapped like a gospel choir as Vinnie marched out with a huge smile on his face. This is what we sang:

> Soon and very soon, we are going to see the King
> Soon and very soon, we are going to see the King
> Soon and very soon, we are going to see the King
> Hallelujah, Hallelujah, we're going to see the King
>
> No more cryin' there, we are going to see the King
> No more cryin' there, we are going to see the King
> No more cryin' there, we are going to see the King
> Hallelujah, Hallelujah, we're going to see the King

> No more dyin' there, we are going to see the King
> No more dyin' there, we are going to see the King
> No more dyin' there, we are going to see the King
> Hallelujah, Hallelujah, we're going to see the King

This is what Vinnie was saying to all of us that day: do not feel sorry for me, for my sacrifice. I make it willingly, and I make it for Jesus. And after all, it is only for a little while. It is only for the rest of my life.

I think what God has been trying to teach me and Carey lately is that we are supposed to see life the way Vinnie did. Our home, the one we have been waiting so long for, is nearly completed now. We are beginning to see that our long wait has not been in vain, and that it will soon bear fruit. Now that the time is short, we find ourselves talking about our home more and more, dreaming about it, picturing our lives there. We know a lot more than we used to about what it will be like, and so it is easier to imagine how things will be when we finally get to move in. We can hardly wait for that day; sometimes we feel that we will burst if we don't get to move in tomorrow. Our current situation is certainly not terrible, and we can tolerate it for as long as we need to. But we are ready, whenever God says we are ready, to go home.

We are also seeing, though, that waiting for our home has been good for us. God had things he wanted to do in our hearts, things which would never have happened if we simply moved straight into our house with no delay. We would have had the right house, but we would not have been the right people. We had growing to do. We needed to wait, to anticipate, and to learn to walk with God in a strange place, so that when we received our home we would still love God more than the place he had prepared for us. God also had things he wanted to do through us. This has been an important time, not only in our lives, but in the lives of people around us, and someday all of us will be eternally grateful that we did not miss out on it. God's plan is absolutely, amazingly perfect in every detail. Knowing this, we would stay like this as long as he asked. Still, we long for our home, and we know that our longing is normal, and right, and good. The house on Neptune is real, after all, and we really are going to live there. It is only a matter of time.

epilogue: arriving on Neptune

The rough draft of this book was written in a time of waiting. While I was re-writing it, though, the house on Neptune was completed, and Carey and I moved in. Everything changed on that day. After months of doing nothing, suddenly there was way too much to do. For several weeks our lives were a flurry of paperwork and boxes and housewarming gifts. We came home from work every day to total chaos, and stayed up late installing blinds and putting together cheap furniture. We were constantly asking each other where things were. Most of our possessions had been in storage for about 8 months, and it was fun to re-discover how we had lived before we became transients. Slowly, as things were put in order, the house began to take shape. At first, it really just felt like another place to sleep, but over time it feels more and more like this place is our home.

The thing that surprised me about moving into our house was this: what I had viewed for so long as the end was really just a beginning. No one told me what an overwhelming thing it is to own a home. For months, Carey and I have thought only about getting to live here, as if that were the goal. Now we see that we are just getting started. I look into the future and I see a never-ending string of things to do: planting a lawn, building shelves in the garage, painting, finding new ways to keep the dog in the yard. In the next couple of years I will have to stain the porch so that the rain doesn't ruin it, and, God willing, re-arrange the office I set up yesterday to make room for a baby. I have not crossed the finish line; I have begun a marathon. This is not a bad thing, though, in fact it's exciting. It is my lawn and my garage and my porch. Of course I should be taking care of them—who else would?

There is also something else happening in the midst of all this activity. In the joyful busyness of the present, we are letting go of the past. Slowly, in some unattended corner of our minds, our other life, in that other house, is beginning to fade from importance. Just a few days ago, it was reality, but now it is only memory. As we are more and more consumed by the delights of our new surroundings, we think less and less about those details that once seemed to dominate all of life, they were so important. I suppose there will come a day when we hardly think about them at all. We will mention them to one another occasionally, and laugh together as we curl up on the couch and bask in the warm glow of one another's company.

I think that is how things will be when we get to heaven. The only thing most of us know about heaven is that we want to get there. That is the goal. Someday, though, we will reach that goal, and it will turn out not to be the end, but a beginning. I believe, or at least hope, that we will be pleasantly surprised by the discovery that there is much to be done. I do not think Jesus saved us simply so that we would get to heaven; he saved us so that we would live there. We will not sit around like guests at an awkward dinner party, for we will be strangers and aliens no more. Heaven is a place to dwell, a place to work and play and discover and enjoy. We belong in heaven; it is our true country. It is our home, and because of that it will always offer us more than enough to do. Once we arrive, there will be too much life to be lived to spend much time dwelling on the past.

The other day I was watching the movie *The Lord of the Rings: The Fellowship of the Ring*, and I was struck by a scene in which Elrond the elf, who is immortal, is remembering an event that took place three thousand years earlier. The film flashes back and forth between that event and the present time, and in both cases his face looks roughly the same; he has not aged at all in three thousand years. In the story, Elrond is a very wise being, and I realized that this makes sense—who wouldn't be wise after three thousand years of living? Then I was reminded of two things at once. One was the song "Amazing Grace," which speaks of a time in heaven "when we've been there ten thousand years," and the other was the first few chapters of Genesis, which record that it used to be common for people to live eight or nine hundred years right here on Earth. A friend and I had been talking just that morning about how much you could accomplish, and what kind of person you might become, if you lived that long. I tried to imagine how wise, loving, joyful, strong, humble, and Christlike we all might be eight hundred, or three thousand, or ten thousand years from now in Heaven. And then I tried to imagine what it will be like to spend not just hundreds or thousands of years living in the presence of God, but forever and ever and ever. My little brain, which has only been around 30 years or so, found this a little overwhelming, but it made me smile nonetheless. We are getting ready to go to our heavenly home, where we will never die. Though I can't fully grasp what that will mean, I know I am glad it's true. I know it makes me want to live differently. I hope it makes me more like the person God meant me to be when he made me, and I hope it does the same for you.

Acknowledgements:

If I know anything about being a writer, it is because of Tom Ready, Fr. Michael Siconolfi, and Dr. Michael Bonin. If I know anything about being a Christian, it is because of my mom, Tim Miller, and Mark Hanke. If I know anything about being a pastor, it is because of Mark and Bard Marshall. If I know anything about being a man, it is because of my brother and my dad.

Many friends were generous with their time and their wisdom, and this book is much better as a result. I'm especially grateful to Joel Dylhoff for his insight when the manuscript was at its roughest, and to Ray Lodge for his help and encouragement in the latter stages of the writing process. Thanks also to Kevin Graves and others who believe in me without any good reason, and to the people of Faith Baptist Church, because of whom I am privileged to be one of those rare people who love their jobs. It's also worth mentioning that I wrote this book on the laptop John Greenlaw gave me. Thanks, John.

Printed in the United States
147098LV00001B/2/P